STOP MAKING CANCER

A RAW VEGAN RECIPE BOOK

STOP MAKING CANCER
A RAW VEGAN RECIPE BOOK

An Oasis of Healing

gatekeeper press
Columbus, Ohio

An Oasis of Healing
Stop Making Cancer
Recipe Book
_____1st Edition_____

Mailing Address:
An Oasis of Healing, PLLC
210 N. Center Street, Suite 102
Mesa, AZ 85201
www.AnOasisofHealing.com
480-834-5414

STOP MAKING CANCER
A Raw Vegan Recipe Book

Published by Gatekeeper Press
2167 Stringtown Rd, Suite 109
Columbus, OH 43123-2989
www.GatekeeperPress.com

ISBN (hardcover): 9781662932762
ISBN (paperback): 9781662932779
eISBN: 9781662932786

Our special thanks to Celena Leland for the preparation
of these recipes and the great care she took to photograph them
so beautifully while working at An Oasis of Healing.
We also thank her for contributing the introduction and new recipes that have
not appeared in previous editions of our recipe book.

This book is dedicated to our patients and those diagnosed with cancer that commit to making the changes necessary to their diet and lifestyle in order to 'Stop Making Cancer'. We admire your strength and determination while undertaking this journey of healing and health restoration.

FOREWORD

By Dr. Thomas Lodi

This process that we call "life" is occurring at an unfathomably dynamic pace. Every second, over 37 million new cells are produced[1], requiring 37 thousand billion biochemical reactions not only to support the production of new cells but to carry out all of the other metabolic requirements.

Hunger exists as a set of physiological and behavioral patterns designed to acquire appropriate nourishment to sustain this magnificent dance of life. These highly complex and precisely coordinated sets of responses are fundamental to the most basic activity of all organisms, from the single-cell bacteria to humans, known as energy homeostasis, i.e., obtaining, using, and maintaining sufficient energy for optimal functioning. The majority of the energy produced by a cell is required simply to maintain the shape or structure of a cell, leaving the remainder for cellular functioning[2,3]. The second impetus to initiate hunger, or the eating response, is when a deficiency in one or more nutrients exists. Nutrients are the basic chemical compounds that make up the structure of cells, tissues, and organs, allowing cells to replace their damaged parts or divide and make a new cell. In addition, nutrients provide the chemicals necessary for the cell to assemble and produce whatever products for which it was designed, e.g., a liver cell producing glutathione for detoxification or a pancreatic cell producing an enzyme for digestion, or a cell in the adrenal gland whose function it is to produce and release cortisol.

It follows that the two internal stimuli that initiate hunger and subsequent feeding behavior through a synchrony of chemical messenger (hormones) and the nervous system are energy and/or nutrient deficiency. Negative energy balance signaling from the gut to the brain occurs when there are low levels of plasma leptin, insulin, and glucose in the blood and high levels of plasma ghrelin and free fatty acids[4]. This combination of hormone and nutrient levels "tells" the brain that there is an energy deficit, which in turn induces the brain to produce chemicals, neurotransmitters, and hormones, that ultimately result in seeking out and eating food. The whole process is exceedingly more complex than simply the relationship between ghrelin, leptin, insulin, glucose, and fatty acids. This combination serves as the final signal to specifically communicate the situation to the brain in order for it to coordinate the adaptive behaviors necessary to restore positive energy and nutrient balance.

Ghrelin, mostly produced in the stomach, is the only hormone circulating in the blood that causes an increase in food intake once it reaches the hypothalamus, a central mediator of internal physiological processes of the body to maintain balance (homeostasis). The hypothalamus signals other areas in the midbrain, including the ventral tegmental area (VTA), which is central to reward recognition, learning, positive emotions, and orgasm[5]. Leptin, produced primarily in fat cells, and insulin from the pancreas, are hormones that increase with eating and inform the brain that it is time to stop eating. Furthermore, low levels of leptin and insulin produce similar effects as high levels of ghrelin through both the hypothalamus (homeostasis center) and the VTA (pleasure). Hence, both homeostatic energy and nutrient balance, as well as pleasure, are required for sufficient eating to occur.

Homeostatic and Hedonic Eating

There are two fundamental and complementary drives or pathways that lead to eating, homeostatic and hedonic. The homeostatic system, as has been discussed, exists as part of the overall survival "instinct", in this case, to maintain sufficient energy and nutrients to carry out living activities. The hedonic pathways are reward-based and are necessary physiological circuits and systems required for learning to occur. Without reward, a particular behavior is unlikely to be repeated. Hedonic pathways can override those associated with homeostasis and is familiar to most as "overeating," that is, eating for pleasure after both energy and nutrient deficits have been replenished. Gone awry, hedonic pathways are responsible for addictive behaviors, not only to food but to drugs, alcohol, which is a drug, gambling, etc., where there are no homeostatic needs to be overridden. In these scenarios, simply pleasure or reward is the motivation. Both drug addiction and the pleasure derived from eating highly desirable and palatable foods share the same neuro-pathways in the limbic system of the brain, specifically the VTA, and a small area within it, the nucleus accumbens, known as the "hedonic hotspot" (pleasure center)[6,7].

Hormones that regulate eating, such as leptin and ghrelin, also regulate the brain's mesolimbic system as a consequence of dopamine (neurotransmitter) signaling, greatly affecting the motivation to obtain food. The mesolimbic system extends from the ventral tegmental area (VTA) and connects to several other structures, the nucleus accumbens, amygdala, hippocampus, and prefrontal cortex[8]. This pathway in the brain mediates pleasure and acts to reward, both essential aspects required for someone to repeat a behavior. Leptin decreases dopamine secretion, inhibiting the activity of certain neurons in the VTA, thereby decreasing pleasure and reward. In contrast, ghrelin stimulates the increase of dopamine secretion in that system, associated with addictive behaviors. Dopamine, along with serotonin, are two chemical messengers in the brain (neurotransmitters) that result in the sensation and perception of pleasure. Whereas ghrelin seems to be associated with homeostatic eating[9], dopamine, endogenous (produced in the body) opiates, and endocannabinoids (brain-produced cannabis-like molecules) mediate hedonic (pleasure) eating. Homeostatic eating has as its goal to replenish energy or nutrient deficits, whereas hedonic eating is the reward and becomes a reinforcer to "do it again."

Both fat and carbohydrates "light up" the 'hedonic hotspot,' whereas protein, i.e., amino acids, do not[10]. Carbohydrates, which stimulate the pancreas to produce insulin, and the low ratio of blood tryptophan (amino acid) to other amino acids that are associated with obesity, act synergistically to increase serotonin levels, hence are very likely to be part of any favorite "comfort food." Tryptophan is the amino acid that serves as the raw material in the body to produce serotonin; hence eating carbohydrates ultimately results in increased serotonin levels. The neurotransmitter serotonin is also a hormone involved with many homeostatic processes such as sleep and digestion but is also the main hormone responsible for feelings of well-being and mood. As stated, serotonin and dopamine mediate pleasure and a sense of emotional well-being.

For these reasons, in our culture, overeating carbohydrates-fat combinations, like potato chips, French fries, pizza, and desserts, makes many people feel better[11] and are known as "comfort foods." Although the cuisine of other cultures may prepare carbohydrate and fat combinations differently, they still rely on the physiology and brain chemistry of pleasure. Of interest, nicotine also increases brain production of serotonin and is partially responsible for its addictive qualities.

Effects of Stress

When mice are experimentally exposed to chronic stressful situations, ghrelin levels increase, as do feeding and weight gain[6]. Moreover, studies with mice demonstrate that ghrelin is associated more with the intake of caloric dense food rather than sweet, more palatable food providing evidence for its relationship to energy homeostasis as opposed to pleasurable eating[9,12]. Furthermore, as much as there is an approximate 25% association between mood disorders and obesity in humans[13], food disorders clearly have an effect on both homeostatic and hedonic eating behavior and vice versa. Eating, by introducing a vast array of different molecules in the form of nutrients, toxic chemicals, insects, and microorganisms, changes the biochemistry of the body, including that of the brain. Hence serotonin, dopamine, endogenous opiates, endo-cannabinoids, and a host of other neurotransmitters modify mood, thinking, emotions, etc. Eating, therefore, has a profound effect not only on overall physiology but also on brain function and psychology.

Happiness, Sadness, and Immunity

It has been firmly established that the immune system is directly affected by emotions and mood[14]. Negative emotions have a direct effect on the endocrine (hormone) system, which produces increases in cortisol, adrenaline, and various immunoglobulins, which in turn decreases overall immunity, just as the stress response. More specifically, the ventral tegmental area (VTA) of the brain, which is involved with positive emotions and reward, or pleasure, when activated, decreases the sympathetic nervous system's activity in the bone marrow, which results in fewer immune suppressor cell (MDSC) production and an increase in both natural killer cells (NK) and activated T-cells followed by a decrease in tumor growth and overall cancer progression[15]. Moreover, stress, depression, and all other negative emotions, including feeling deprived and sad, have the opposite effect of depressing the immune system and supporting tumor progression[16,17].

Eat, Drink and Be Merry

The ancient advice of King Solomon, from Ecclesiastes[18], has a profundity that most do not appreciate. Medical science has advanced our understanding of the two-way interactions and mutual effects of the mind and body, specifically the effects of the mind on the immune system. Although eating for pleasure can override eating for health, resulting in deleterious effects such as obesity and chronic illnesses including cancer, without the pleasure of eating, the effects can be as devastating. Therefore, just as it is essential to balance all of the homeostatic systems in the body, so is it essential to recognize and respect the need for pleasurable eating. It is simply not enough to know what constitutes a healthy diet since human beings, more than any other creatures, are driven by pleasure with regards to eating.

Appetite vs. Hunger

Hunger, as has been discussed, is a set of physiological responses to nutrient or energy deficits, and all of the behaviors associated with satisfying those needs do not require learning; they are instinctual.

Appetite, on the other hand, arises from memory and associative thinking (mind) rather than physiology; hence, in that respect, appetite can never be satisfied. Furthermore, they are learned. When children younger than the age of three years are fed foods before their minds have developed, these foods become directly associated with the physiology of hunger and serve as the basis of appetite as the mind develops. Appetites can and are modified throughout life as long as the "new food" results in dopamine release in the brain and pleasure is derived. As has been discussed, the neurochemicals and hormones associated with pleasure enhance the immune system, as well as produce a sense of overall well-being. The challenge in all of this is how to make food that is homeostatically sound, as well as pleasurable. Homeostatic eating, as will be recalled, is initiated by nutrient and/or energy deficits; hence the food ingested from this physiological drive must supply these deficient nutrients and energy. Since humans are raised being fed foods appropriate to their culture rather than being fed foods directed by instinct, as occurs with animals, the academic field of nutrition has developed, hoping that knowledge will override "desire" or "appetite." We at An Oasis of Healing have learned over the past 17 years just how powerful appetite is and that it must be respected and brought into a methodology for changing one's food preferences and eating practices where food can be enjoyed, and also fulfill the energy and nutrient deficits required to restore homeostasis.

We offer this new recipe book in support of this truth, "if it does not taste good, it is not good for us."

Thomas Lodi, MD, MDH
Founder of An Oasis of Healing, PLC

References

1. Scientific American. Our Bodies Replace Billions of Cells Every Day. https://www.scientificamerican.com/article/our-bodies-replace-billions-of-cells-every-day/, accessed Jan 20, 2021.
2. Thomas N. Seyfried, Gabriel Arismendi-Morillo, Purna Mukherjee, Christos Chinopoulos, On the Origin of ATP Synthesis in Cancer Open AccessPublished: October 31, 2020DOI: https://doi.org/10.1016/j.isci.2020.101761
3. Veech RL, King MT, Pawlosky R, Bradshaw PC, Curtis W. Relationship between inorganic ion distribution, resting membrane potential, and the $\Delta G'$ of ATP hydrolysis: a new paradigm. FASEB J. 2019;33(12):13126-13130. doi:10.1096/fj.201901942R
4. Lockie SH, Andrews ZB. The hormonal signature of energy deficit: Increasing the value of food reward. Mol Metab. 2013;2(4):329-336. Published 2013 Aug 19. doi:10.1016/j.molmet.2013.08.003
5. Holstege G, Georgiadis JR, Paans AM, Meiners LC, van der Graaf FH, Reinders AA (October 2003). "Brain activation during human male ejaculation". The Journal of Neuroscience. 23 (27): 9185–93. doi:10.1523/JNEUROSCI.23-27-09185.2003. PMC 6740826. PMID 14534252.
6. Lutter M, Nestler EJ. Homeostatic and hedonic signals interact in the regulation of food intake. J Nutr. 2009;139(3):629-632. doi:10.3945/jn.108.097618
7. Castro DC, Berridge KC. Opioid hedonic hotspot in nucleus accumbens shell: mu, delta, and kappa maps for enhancement of sweetness "liking" and "wanting". J Neurosci. 2014 Mar 19;34(12):4239-50. doi: 10.1523/JNEUROSCI.4458-13.2014. PMID: 24647944; PMCID: PMC3960467.
8. Will M.J., Franzblau E.B., Kelley A.E. Nucleus accumbens mu-opioids regulate intake of a high-fat diet via activation of a distributed brain network. Journal of Neuroscience. 2003;23(7):2882–2888.
9. Bomberg E.M. Central ghrelin induces feeding driven by energy needs not by reward. Neuroreport. 2007;18(6):591–595
10. Pecina S., Berridge K.C. Hedonic hot spot in nucleus accumbens shell: where do mu-opioids cause increased hedonic impact of sweetness? Journal of Neuroscience. 2005;25(50):11777–11786.
11. Wurtman RJ, Wurtman JJ. Brain serotonin, carbohydrate-craving, obesity and depression. Obes Res. 1995 Nov;3 Suppl 4:477S-480S. doi: 10.1002/j.1550-8528.1995.tb00215.x. PMID: 8697046.
12. Overduin J. Ghrelin increases the motivation to eat but does not alter food palatability. American Journal of Physiology-Regulatory Integrative and Comparative Physiology. 2012;303(3):R259–R269.
13. Simon GE, Von Korff M, Saunders K, Miglioretti DL, Crane PK, van Belle G, Kessler RC. Association between obesity and psychiatric disorders in the US adult population. Arch Gen Psychiatry. 2006 Jul;63(7):824-30. doi: 10.1001/archpsyc.63.7.824. PMID: 16818872; PMCID: PMC1913935.
14. Barak Y. The immune system and happiness. Autoimmun Rev. 2006 Oct;5(8):523-7. doi: 10.1016/j.autrev.2006.02.010. Epub 2006 Mar 21. PMID: 17027886.
15. Ben-Shaanan, T.L., Schiller, M., Azulay-Debby, H. et al. Modulation of anti-tumor immunity by the brain's reward system. Nat Commun 9, 2723 (2018). https://doi.org/10.1038/s41467-018-05283-5
16. Spiegel, D., Sands, S. & Koopman, C. Pain and depression in patients with cancer. Cancer 74, 2570–2578 (1994).
17. Giese-Davis, J. et al. Decrease in depression symptoms is associated with longer survival in patients with metastatic breast cancer: a secondary analysis. J. Clin. Oncol. 29, 413–420 (2011).
18. Bible Hub. Ecclesiastes 8:15. https://www.biblehub.com/ecclesiastes/8-15.htm, accessed Mar 10, 2021.

CONTENTS

INTRODUCTION

Welcome to Raw Cuisine

There is no greater treasure in life than good health, and the best way to protect our health is by consuming foods that strengthen our body's natural healing abilities. Nature offers us everything we need to accomplish this: fresh fruits, vegetables, nuts, seeds, and sprouts that provide an abundance of vital nutrients. The nutrients in these foods work synergistically to support optimal health, and when any of those nutrients are destroyed, the natural harmony of the food is lost.

The purpose of raw cuisine is to preserve the healthful qualities of food by ensuring none of the delicate vitamins, enzymes, or phytochemicals are lost to heat and oxidation. These nutrients are what allow your body to produce energy, reduce inflammation, protect healthy cells, and break down cancerous cells. The nutritional density of raw, living, plant-based foods is what gives this diet its therapeutic value, which is why this lifestyle is an integral part of our cancer program at An Oasis of Healing.

In order to enjoy good health, it is important to nourish yourself each and every day. When you are in the process of healing from disease, the necessity of a nutrient-rich diet becomes paramount. But if you are new to raw vegan cuisine, you may be wondering where to start. This recipe book will be your guide as you begin reshaping your diet. Here are some important things to keep in mind:

» Cooking reduces the nutritional value of food by denaturing vitamins and enzymes, so raw foods are never heated above 105 to 115 degrees Fahrenheit.
» Animal foods are acid-forming and can be inflammatory, whereas vegetables are alkaline and anti-inflammatory.
» The amount of nutrients you absorb from food depends on your digestive function. Juicing, fasting, and consuming fermented foods are excellent ways to enhance your gut health.

Learning how to prepare raw food takes some practice, but with the proper techniques you can achieve a wide variety of textures and flavors to satisfy any craving. Fresh and vibrant or hearty and comforting—it is all possible with raw foods!

Tips for Transitioning

Embarking on a new lifestyle can come with challenges, but if you prepare accordingly you will find the transition to be smooth and rewarding. To assist you in getting started, we have included a few tips:

1. It is important to keep in mind that many raw foods are less calorically dense than the foods you are used to. To help ensure that you are meeting your caloric needs, be sure to consume fat-rich foods like nuts, seeds, avocados, and coconut.

2. Having snack options on hand at all times helps keep you on track. Make some big batches of raw food staples like flackers, kale chips, energy chunks, and coconut yogurt.

3. Learning how to mimic your favorite comfort foods goes a long way in helping you feel satisfied. In this book we have recipes for tacos, mac and cheese, bagels, pizza, and more!

4. For those with impaired digestion, switching from a mostly cooked diet to a completely raw diet can cause gastrointestinal distress. For this reason, we recommend slowly incorporating more fresh, living foods over the course of several weeks, and consider taking digestive enzymes if needed.

5. Probiotics are great for supporting gut health and helping you process all the fiber in vegetables. Be sure to do your research and find a reputable brand.

Useful Equipment

Having the right equipment in your kitchen makes raw food prep quick, easy, and enjoyable. You will need the basics—like sharp knives, a cutting board, and large bowls—but you might also want to consider investing in these useful tools:

Dehydrator

The dehydrator is another kitchen essential for the raw food lifestyle because it expands the possibilities of what you can make. We will talk more about dehydrating later, but for now it is important to know what kind of dehydrator to look for. You'll notice there are two options available: the stackable type and the box type. Stackable dehydrators (also called vertical flow dehydrators) are generally smaller and more affordable, but their design limits the size and shape of what you can put in them. Also, their heat distribution tends to be uneven, making them less effective. Box dehydrators (also called horizontal flow dehydrators) can accommodate a much wider variety of foods and produce more consistent results. Having any dehydrator is better than not having one at all, but if you have the option we recommend you choose a box dehydrator.

High power blender

A high power blender (like a Vitamix, Ninja, or Blendtec) is one of the most essential kitchen tools you can own. The blades spin faster and with much greater force than regular blenders, making it easy to blend just about anything. In our kitchen we use high power blenders for smoothies, nut milks, nut cheeses, dips, dressings, soups, sauces, and desserts. Throughout this recipe book, you'll see that we call for the use of a blender often, and we recommend that you use one that is high powered.

Food processor

Second to having a good blender is having a food processor. Food processors reduce the amount of time you spend chopping nuts and veggies, and they are great for blending up mixtures that are too thick for the blender. Food processors produce a coarse texture, which is perfect for things like nut breads, veggie burgers, pates, certain nut cheeses, and many desserts.

Countertop Juicer

Juicing is another topic we will touch on later, but here we will share what you need to know about choosing a good juicer. As you shop around you will notice that the most common types of juicers are centrifugal, masticating, and twin gear.

Centrifugal juicers work by shredding vegetables with a fast spinning grater and forcing the juice through a straining basket. This process produces juice quickly, but it also generates a lot of heat and oxidation, which damages delicate nutrients and enzymes.

Masticating juicers use a slow spinning auger to crush vegetables into a pulp, which is run through a strainer to extract the juice. This process takes longer, but it produces a high-quality juice.

Twin gear juicers use two augers to crush vegetables and press the pulp into a strainer to extract the juice. This type of juicer is the largest and most expensive, but it produces the most nutrient-dense juice.

There are pros and cons to each, and the choice is ultimately up to you. However, we discourage the use of centrifugal juicers, as they produce the least nutritious juice.

Straining Bags

Straining bags are nothing fancy, but they are very useful in a raw food kitchen. They can be used to make nut milks and to grow sprouts, two things which we do almost daily at An Oasis of Healing. We recommend getting one or two natural-fiber straining bags so that you can make the most of your raw food lifestyle.

Exceptions to Raw

While a major part of your diet should consist of raw foods, we recognize that there are a few exceptions. For instance, mushrooms are a food that should be cooked for safety and for maximum nutrient absorption. You will see that any recipe in this book that contains mushrooms gives instructions on how to cook them. Another exception is tempeh; we love organic tempeh because it is a fermented food which offers a great deal of protein and phytonutrients. It is made from cooked soybeans, but we include it in our recipes for its health benefits and culinary properties.

Other exceptions include things like toasted sesame oil, smoked paprika, and pasteurized items like tamari and canned coconut cream. These ingredients do not have much nutritive value but they add a lot of flavor, even when used in small amounts.

Dehydrating

When you dive into the raw food lifestyle, you will find that a dehydrator allows you to create a wide variety of textures and flavors that would not otherwise be possible. You will notice that the recipes in this book give a wide range for dehydrating times. This is because dehydration is sensitive to many variables, including the moisture of your ingredients and the climate that you live in. Fortunately, dehydrated foods are pretty forgiving, so feel free to play around with the times and find out what works for you.

Fermenting

Lacto-fermentation is a process that has been used throughout history by people of all cultures. It serves many purposes, from preserving food, to deepening the complexity of flavors, to aiding in digestion. These properties are all made possible by two essential ingredients: microbes and time.

Some fermented foods utilize the microbes that are naturally present on the food and in the air, others rely on probiotics to get things started in the right direction. In either case, the specific microbe that does most of the work is a type of bacteria called lactobacillus, which breaks down food by converting sugars into lactic acid. This not only gives fermented food its characteristic flavor, it also preserves nutrients and provides an environment that is inhospitable to harmful bacteria. And because fermented foods are partially broken down, they are easier to digest.

Raw cuisine utilizes lacto-fermentation in the making of coconut yogurt, nut cheeses, and sauerkraut. Each one can be a wonderful addition to any meal. In fact, we recommend incorporating fermented foods into your daily menu, so that you get a natural dose of probiotics each day.

Juicing

The centerpiece of our raw food lifestyle is fresh, vibrant green juice. Green juice is made by extracting the nutrient-rich liquid from fresh green vegetables, and removing the fiber in the process. Fiber is an essential part of a healthy diet, but juicing allows you to consume a much larger quantity of produce than would otherwise be possible. The absence of fiber also allows you to quickly absorb the vitamins, minerals, and beneficial phytonutrients, without putting a strain on your digestive system. You can think of green juice as a natural (and delicious!) liquid multivitamin.

When purchasing green juice from a store or restaurant, be sure that it is high quality! It should be freshly made, light on fruit, and organic. It is also important to check the ingredient list and make sure that it does not contain any additives.

Soaking Nuts and Seeds

Soaking nuts and seeds is an important part of the raw food lifestyle. These foods are high in healthy fat, protein, and minerals, but they also contain high amounts of phytic acid, a compound which is often referred to as an anti-nutrient because it binds to and inhibits the absorption of certain minerals.

Because nuts and seeds make up a large part of a raw diet, it is necessary to take the extra step to ensure that they are properly prepared. Soak your nuts and seeds for the appropriate amount of time, then drain and rinse them. Spread them in a single layer on a dehydrator sheet and dehydrate at 105 °F until completely dry (this can take anywhere between one to two days). After they have been dehydrated you can store them in a cool dark place for a month (or longer if kept in the refrigerator).

A note on soaking nuts before blending:
If you do not have a high power blender, we recommend soaking your nuts and seeds (and not dehydrating them) prior to blending. This makes them easier to blend.

Sprouting

Sprouts are rich in Vitamins A, B, C, and K, as well as a variety of enzymes, minerals, and amino acids. Most sprouts can be grown in jars or straining bags; all you have to do is soak your seeds, grains, or legumes for the appropriate amount of time, then drain and rinse them. Place them in a straining bag or a jar with a sprouting lid and let them sit at room temperature, rinsing twice a day until they grow tails (this can take between one to three days), then you can store them in the refrigerator for up to one week.

Check out our soaking and sprouting chart on page 7.

SEED	SOAK TIME	SPROUT TIME
Almonds	8-10 hours	None
Adzuki beans	14-16 hours	3-5 days
Amaranth	1 hour	1-3 days
Brazil Nuts	2-4 hours	None
Broccoli seeds	6-8 hours	2-4 days
Buckwheat	1 hour	1-2 days
Cashews	6-8 hours	None
Chickpeas	16-18 hours	2-4 days
Lentils	4-6 hours	2-3 days
Macadamia	2-4 hours	None
Mung beans	14-16 hours	3-5 days
Oat groats	16-18 hours	1-2 days
Pecans	6-8 hours	None
Pistachios	4-6 hours	None
Pumpkin seeds	6-8 hours	1-2 days
Sesame seeds	4-6 hours	1-2 days
Sunflower seeds	6-8 hours	3-5 days (in soil)
Quinoa	2-4 hours	1-3 days
Walnuts	6-8 hours	None
Wheat berries	10-12 hours	3-5 days (in soil)
Wild rice	8-10 hours	3-5 days

BREAKFASTS

Green Juice	11
Nut Milks	12
Berry Smoothie	14
Chocolate Shake	15
Coconut Yogurt	17
Nutnola	18
Buckwheaties	20
Sprouted Oatmeal	21
Chia Pudding	23
Crepes: Two ways	25

GREEN JUICE

Makes: 1 Quart • Prep time: 20 minutes • Total time: 20 minutes

1 bunch lacinato kale

4 handfuls spinach

2 cucumbers

⅓ head of celery

1 green apple

½-1 lemon (with rind)

¼-½ bunch parsley

1 thumb ginger

Wash and cut all produce to an appropriate size for your juicer. Feed produce into the juicer, alternating between ingredients to prevent clogging.

Taste your juice and adjust the flavors accordingly:

» Lemon and ginger add zest

» Parsley adds complexity

» Celery adds depth

» Cucumber rounds out the flavors

Drink your juice soon after making it to avoid oxidation. Otherwise, cover tightly and store in the refrigerator for up to one day.

NUT MILKS

Makes: 1 Quart • Prep time: 10 minutes • Total time: 10 minutes

Almond Milk:

1 cup almonds

4 cups water

Hemp Milk*:

3/4 cup hemp seeds

4 cups water

Pecan Milk*:

1 cup pecans

4 cups water

Coconut Milk:

1 cup dried coconut (unsweetened)

4 cups water

Oat Milk:

1 cup gluten-free oats

4 cups water

Cashew Cream*:

2 cups cashews

2 cups water

Place your ingredients in a blender and blend on high for 30 seconds or longer (depending on the power of your blender).

Pour mixture into a straining bag. Strain the mixture by twisting the top of the bag closed with one hand and squeezing the bag with the other hand.

Store in the refrigerator for up to three days (separation is normal).

*Some milks do not require straining.

BERRY SMOOTHIE

Basic Recipe:

1 ½ cup unsweetened nut milk	1 Tbsp flax or chia seed
½ cup fresh or frozen berries	1 handful of spinach
2 Tbsp hemp seed	Pinch of salt

Optional Extras:

1 Tbsp sacha inchi powder	½ tsp amla powder
1 tsp medicinal mushroom powder	¼ tsp ashwagandha powder
½ tsp maca powder	¼ turmeric powder

Place the ingredients in a blender and blend on medium-high until smooth.

We recommend adding one or two of the "super food" powders listed above, as they are extremely nutrient dense. Some of them have a bitter flavor, so you may want to add a drop of stevia or a splash of coconut water to sweeten things up.

Taste your creation and make adjustments as necessary. Drink immediately, or cover tightly and store in the refrigerator for up to six hours.

CHOCOLATE SHAKE

Makes: 16 oz • Prep time: 10 minutes • Total time: 10 minutes

Basic Recipe:

½ cup young Thai coconut meat

½ cup coconut water

1 cup filtered water

1 Tbsp cacao powder

½ Medjool date, pitted

Pinch of salt

Optional Extras:

1 Tbsp sacha inchi powder

1 Tbsp almond butter

1 Tbsp hemp seed

1 tsp medicinal mushroom powder

½ tsp maca powder

½ tsp amla powder

Place the ingredients in a blender and blend on medium-high until smooth. This may take longer than your typical smoothie, depending on how mature the coconut meat is.

For extra protein and nutrients, consider adding some ingredients from the "optional extras" list. And if you would prefer, you can switch out the Medjool date for stevia.

Taste your creation and make adjustments as necessary. Drink immediately, or cover tightly and store in the refrigerator for up to one day.

COCONUT YOGURT

Makes: 3-4 cups • Prep time: 30 minutes • Total time: 1-2 days

3 cups young Thai coconut meat

1-2 cups fresh coconut water

Contents of 1 probiotic capsule

Place coconut meat and coconut water in a blender and blend on high until smooth (this may take a few minutes). Add more coconut water if you prefer a thinner consistency. Add the probiotic and blend on low to combine.

Place the yogurt in a large jar, filling no more than ¾ of the way full (as it will bubble up while it ferments, filling with gas produced by the good bacteria). Cover with a clean towel and leave at room temperature for 18-36 hours. The longer it sits, the more tangy it will become.

Once it reaches your preferred level of fermentation, cover tightly and store in the refrigerator. Note that it will thicken up a little bit as it cools.

During the winter, the fermentation may take longer. To speed things up you can place your jar in the oven with the light on. This creates a slightly warm environment for a perfect fermentation—just be sure the oven has not been used recently!

Tip: you can make kefir by adding a probiotic to the leftover coconut water and leaving it out to ferment.

NUTNOLA

Makes: 2 cups • Prep time: 10 minutes • Total time: 16-18 hours

For the base:

½ cup almonds

½ cup walnuts

½ cup pecans

½ cup coconut flakes (unsweetened)

2 Tbsp pumpkin seeds

2 Tbsp hemp seeds

For the coating:

⅓ cup water

1 Medjool date, pitted

2 tsp cinnamon

½ tsp vanilla

Pinch of salt

Place all nuts in a food processor and pulse a few times. Add seeds and coconut flakes, pulse again.

In a blender, combine the coating ingredients and blend until smooth. Feel free to add some "super food" powders to the mix, like maca or reishi powder.

Pour the coating over the nut mixture and pulse to combine. Spread mixture onto a Teflex sheet and dehydrate at 110 °F for 16-18 hours.

Serve over coconut yogurt or topped with your favorite nut milk.

Store in an airtight container for up to one month.

BUCKWHEATIES

Makes: 4 cups • Prep time: 10 minutes • Total time: 2-3 days

Basic Recipe:

4 cups buckwheat groats   8 cups filtered water

Optional Extras:

½ cup nuts and seeds   ¼ cup coconut flakes (unsweetened)

¼ cup goji berries   2 tsp cinnamon

Soak buckwheat groats in water for about 1 hour. Drain and rinse thoroghly (this can be done in a mesh colander or a straining bag). To sprout, let them sit at room temperature for 1-2 days, rinsing twice a day.

Once they've sprouted ¼-inch tails, spread them onto a Teflex sheet and dehydrate at 105 °F for 12-14 hours.

Add any extra ingredients you would like. Serve over coconut yogurt or topped with your favorite nut milk.

Store in an airtight container for up to one month.

SPROUTED OATMEAL

Makes: 4 cups • Prep time: 20 minutes • Total time: 2-3 days

Basic Recipe:

1 ½ cups oat groats   4 cups filtered water

Optional Extras:

1 cup nut milk   1 tsp chia seeds

¼ cup nuts and seeds   1 tsp cinnamon

¼ cup berries   ½ tsp vanilla

Soak oat groats in water for 16-18 hours. Drain and rinse thoroghly (this can be done in a mesh colander, a jar with a sprouting lid, or a straining bag). To sprout, let them sit at room temperature for 1-2 days, rinsing twice a day.

Once the oats have sprouted ¼-inch tails, put them in an airtight container and keep in the refrigerator until ready to use. Whole sprouted oats last up to one week.

To prepare oatmeal, place sprouted oats in a food processor with nut milk and process until it reaches the consistency of steel cut oats. Add additional nut milk if necessary, along with any extra ingredients you would like.

Serve immediately, or cover tightly and keep in the refrigerator for up to one day.

CHIA PUDDING

Makes: 1 serving • Prep time: 5 minutes • Total time: 30 minutes

Basic recipe:

1 cup plant-based milk   2-4 Tbsp chia seeds

Optional extras:

½ tsp vanilla   1 Tbsp almond butter

¼ tsp cinnamon   1 Tbsp berries

¼ tsp maca powder   1-2 drops stevia

Mix the plant-based milk and chia seeds together in a jar or bowl. Let sit for at least 20 minutes, stirring frequently for the first few minutes (to avoid clumping). Add any additional ingredients you would like.

Enjoy immediately or cover tightly and store in the refrigerator for up to three days.

CREPES: TWO WAYS

For the wraps:

¾ cup coconut meat

½ cup flax seed, ground

1 cup water

½ tsp salt

For savory filling:

2 cups mushrooms, sliced

1 cup broccoli, finely chopped

¼ cup tahini

2 Tbsp water

1 Tbsp lemon juice

1 Tbsp coconut aminos

2 tsp chickpea miso

1 clove garlic, minced

Black pepper to taste

Nutritional yeast to taste

For sweet filling:

1 cup berries

¾ cup coconut yogurt

¼ cup coconut butter

½ cup pecans, chopped

Place the ingredients for the wraps in a blender and blend on high until smooth. Pour ⅓ cup portions onto Teflex sheets and spread into circles between ⅛- and ¼-inch thick. Dehydrate at 105 °F for 5-8 hours, flipping halfway through. If the edges become crispy, brush with water to rehydrate.

If not using immediately, allow wraps to dehydrate completely. When ready to use, dip each wrap in water and place back in the dehydrator for about 20 minutes.

For savory filling:

Place mushrooms in a saucepan with a pinch of salt and just enough water to cover them. Bring to a boil and cook for about five minutes. Remove from heat, drain, and let cool.

Place the broccoli in a food processor and pulse into small pieces. Transfer to a bowl and mix in the mushrooms.

In a small bowl, whisk together tahini, water, lemon juice, coconut aminos, chickpea miso, garlic, black pepper, and nutritional yeast. Pour this mixture over the broccoli and mushrooms; toss to combine.

Spoon mixture into wraps and fold closed. Top with parsley or green onions if desired. Serve immediately.

....

For sweet filling:

In a bowl, mash together berries, coconut yogurt, and coconut butter using a fork or pastry blender.

Spoon mixture into your wraps, sprinkle with chopped pecans, and fold closed. Top with almond butter, additional berries, or cinnamon if desired. Serve immediately.

BREADS AND CRACKERS

FLACKERS

Makes: 1 tray • Prep time: 5 minutes • Total time: 20-24 hours

Basic Recipe:

1 cup flax seed

2 cups water

Tomato-basil*:

1 cup tomato, blended

½ cup fresh basil, chopped

¼ tsp salt

Dash of black pepper

Cilantro-jalapeno:

½ cup fresh cilantro, chopped

1 small jalapeno, minced

¼ tsp salt

Dash of cumin

Dill-chive:

2 Tbsp fresh dill (or 1 Tbsp dried)

3 Tbsp fresh chives (or 2 Tbsp dried)

1 glove garlic, minced

¼ tsp salt

Seeded:

2 Tbsp pumpkin seeds

2 Tbsp sunflower seeds

1 Tbsp sesame seeds

½ tsp salt

Mix all ingredients of your choice together and let sit for 1-3 hours to soak, stirring occasionally.

Once the flax has absorbed the water, spread mixture ¼-inch thick on a Teflex sheet. Score into squares with a butter knife and dehydrate at 110 °F for 20-24 hours, or until completely dry. Store in a sealed container at room temperature.

*For the tomato-basil flackers, subtract 1 cup of water from the basic recipe, as this will be replaced by 1 cup of tomato purée.

CRUCIFEROUS CRACKERS

Makes: 2 trays • Prep time: 15 minutes • Total time: 20-24 hours

2 cups broccoli or cauliflower
1 cup flax seed
1 cup water

½ cup sunflower seeds
2 Tbsp Italian seasoning
1 tsp salt

Place all ingredients in a food processor and process until the broccoli or cauliflower is finely ground (the seeds may not be completely ground—that's okay). Let mixture sit for about 10 minutes to thicken up.

Pour mixture onto a Teflex sheet and spread to ¼-inch thick. Score into squares with a butter knife and dehydrate at 110 °F for 20-24 hours, or until completely dry.

Feel free to play around with this recipe! Add some sundried tomatoes, garlic, onions, or nutritional yeast. Or try a different flavor profile, like dill, parsley, and shredded carrot. Get creative!

Store in a sealed container at room temperature for up to two weeks.

TORTILLA CHIPS

Makes: 36 chips • Prep time: 15 minutes • Total time: 22-24 hours

2 cup cauliflower, chopped

1 cup corn, fresh or frozen

½ cup onion

¼ cup flax seed, ground

1-2 Tbsp nutritional yeast (optional)

1 clove garlic

1 tsp salt

½ tsp black pepper

Place all ingredients in a food processor and process until mostly smooth.

Scoop ⅓ cup portions onto Teflex sheets and spread into 5-inch circles between ⅛- and ¼-inch thick.

Dehydrate at 115 °F for 22-24 hours, or until crispy. Cut each tortilla into 6 triangular sections to create chips (this can be done before or after they are fully dehydrated).

Try these tortilla chips with fresh salsa, guacamole, or nacho "cheese!"

Store in a sealed container at room temperature for up to one week.

ONION BREAD

Makes: 1 tray • Prep time: 20 minutes • Total time: 20-24 hours

1 cup yellow onion, diced

1 cup sunflower seeds

1 cup almonds

¼ cup ground flax seed

¼ cup tamari

¼ cup water

In a food processor, combine ½ cup onion with remaining ingredients and process until smooth. Add remaining onions and gently pulse to combine, leaving visible chunks.

Pour mixture onto a Teflex sheet. Spread to about ½-inch thick, score into squares using a butter knife, and dehydrate at 110 °F for 20-24 hours, flipping onto a mesh tray after the first few hours.

Store in a sealed container in the refrigerator for up to one week.

BASIC BUNS

1 medium zucchini, peeled

2 cups almonds

⅓ cup flax seed, ground

⅓ cup water

3 Tbsp coconut aminos

Pinch of salt

In a food processor, process zucchini until very finely chopped. Add almonds and process until smooth. Add remaining ingredients and process for about one minute, until it starts to become fluffy.

Scoop ⅓ cup portions onto a Teflex sheet and shape into buns, about 1-inch thick. Dehydrate at 105 °F for 40-48 hours, transferring to a mesh tray after the first few hours.

Serve with olive oil or coconut butter, or as a side for soups and chili.

Store in a sealed container in the refrigerator for up to one week.

ITALIAN HERB LOAF

Makes: 5-inch loaf · Prep time: 20 minutes · Total time: 18-22 hours

1 cup almonds	¼ cup hemp seeds
1 cup walnuts or pecans	2 Tbsp flax seed, ground
½ cup zucchini, roughly chopped	2 Tbsp fresh Italian herbs (1 Tbsp dried)
⅓ cup water	1 tsp salt
¼ cup onion, roughly chopped	½ tsp garlic powder
¼ cup sun-dried tomato, chopped	2 Tbsp Brazil nut parmesan (optional)

Place nuts, zucchini, and water in a food processor and process into a thick, slightly grainy dough. Add all remaining ingredients except Brazil nut parmesan, and process to combine.

Pour mixture onto a Teflex sheet and form into a loaf, about 5 inches long, 2 inches thick, and 3 inches wide. Top with Brazil nut parmesan (if using), cut into 6 slices and dehydrate at 105 °F for 18-22 hours. Transfer to a mesh tray after the first few hours.

Note: You can use chopped cauliflower or shredded yam in place of zucchini.

Store in a sealed container in the refrigerator for up to one week.

SANDWICH BREAD

Makes: 1 tray • Prep time: 20 minutes • Total time: 20-24 hours

¼ cup onion, roughly chopped
¼ cup tomato, roughly chopped
¼ cup zucchini, roughly chopped
1 cup walnuts

½ cup sunflower seeds
½ cup pumpkin seeds
¼ cup flax seed, ground
1 tsp salt

Place onion, tomato, and zucchini in a food processor and process until mostly smooth. Add nuts, seeds, and salt and process until it forms a slightly grainy dough. You may need to add a splash of water to achieve this texture.

Pour dough onto a Teflex sheet and spread to about ½-inch thick. Score into squares using a butter knife and dehydrate at 110 °F for 20-24 hours, flipping onto a mesh tray after the first few hours.

Serve with avocado, lettuce, tomato, or any of your favorite sandwich fixings!

Store in a sealed container in the refrigerator for up to one week.

GARLIC BREADSTICKS

Makes: 6 sticks • Prep time: 20 minutes • Total time: 24-26 hours

For the breadsticks:

1 medium zucchini, peeled

1 ½ cup Brazil nuts

2 Tbsp flax seed, ground

1 Tbsp coconut aminos

½ tsp garlic powder

½ tsp salt

For the topping:

2 Tbsp nutritional yeast

2 cloves garlic, minced

1 tsp Italian seasoning

Pinch of salt

Place zucchini in a food processor and grind into small pieces. Add all remaining ingredients and process until smooth and fluffy.

Divide the mixture into six portions and shape them into sticks. Place on a Teflex sheet and coat each stick with the topping.

Dehydrate at 105 °F for 24-26 hours, transferring to a mesh tray after the first few hours.

Store in a sealed container in the refrigerator for up to one week.

EVERYTHING BAGELS

Makes: 8 bagels • Prep time: 20 minutes • Total time: 20-22 hours

1 medium zucchini	¼ cup water
¾ cup almonds	3 Tbsp flax seed, ground
½ cup walnuts	2 Tbsp coconut aminos
½ cup pecans	¼ tsp garlic powder
¼ cup sunflower seeds	½ tsp salt
¼ cup pumpkin seeds	¼ cup "everything bagel" seasoning

In a food processor, grind zucchini into small pieces. Add remaining ingredients (except "everything bagel" seasoning) and process into a thick, slightly grainy dough.

Scoop ¼-cup portions onto a Teflex sheet. Shape into ½-inch thick discs, and make a hole in the center of each one using your finger. Top with bagel seasoning (if using), or substitute with sesame seeds, poppy seeds, or any topping of your choice. Dehydrate at 110 °F for 20-22 hours, transfering to a mesh dehydrator tray after the first 1-2 hours.

Serve with coconut-cashew cream cheese!

Store in a sealed container in the refrigerator for up to one week.

TOMATO-BASIL WRAPS

Makes: 6 wraps · Prep time: 30 minutes · Total time: 16-18 hours

2 cup tomatoes, chopped	¼ cup sundried tomatoes
1 cups water	1 clove garlic
¾ cup flax seeds	1 tsp salt
½ cup young Thai coconut meat	¼ cup fresh basil, chopped

In a high-power blender, blend all ingredients except basil until smooth (this mixture is very thick, so you may have to use your blender's tamper tool). Transfer to a bowl and fold in basil.

Scoop ½-cup portions onto Teflex sheets, spreading into 7-8 inch circles, between ⅛- and ¼-inch thick. Dehydrate at 105 °F for 16-18 hours, or until dry but pliable.

If they get crispy, dip in water and place back in the dehydrator for 20 minutes.

Fill with chickenless salad (page 67) or veggies and hummus (pages 53 and 54).

To store, dehydrate completely and store in a sealed container at room temperature for up to a week. When ready to use, dip each one in water and return to the dehydrator for 20 minutes.

NUT CHEESES, DIPS, AND SPREADS

ALMOND-CASHEW CHEESE WHEEL

Makes: 1.5 cups • Prep time: 30 minutes • Total time: 2+ days

1 cup cashews

1 cup almonds*

¾ cup water

½ tsp salt

1 clove garlic

Contents of 1 probiotic capsule

2 Tbsp dried herbs

In a high-power blender, combine all ingredients except probiotic. Blend on high until smooth (this may take a few minutes, and will probably require you to use the tamper tool as you blend). Empty the contents of the probiotic capsule into the mixture and blend on low to combine.

Pour mixture into a bowl and cover with a clean towel. Let sit at room temperature overnight, or up to eight days. The longer it ferments, the more complex and cheesey the flavors become.

Once the nut cheese has fermented to your liking, place it in the refrigerator overnight to set.

To shape the cheese, first scrape the dried layer off the top. Scoop the cheese mixture onto a piece of parchment paper, shape into a wheel, and coat with your favorite dried herbs.

Store in a sealed container in the refrigerator for up to three weeks.

*For a super smooth texture, soak and peel the almonds before blending.

COCONUT-CASHEW CREAM CHEESE

Makes: 1.5 cups • Prep time: 10 minutes • Total time: 18-24 hours

1 cup cashews

½ cup water

½ cup raw, cultured coconut yogurt*

¼ tsp salt

In a high-power blender, blend cashews, water, and salt on high until smooth (you may have to use the tamper tool). Add coconut yogurt and blend on low to combine.

Pour mixture into a bowl and cover with a clean towel. Let sit at room temperature overnight, until tangy enough for your liking. Feel free to jazz it up by adding your favorite herbs and spices.

Store in a sealed container in the refrigerator for up to two weeks.

*Be sure that your yogurt is raw and cultured, not pasteurized. The cultures in your yogurt act as the starter to ferment this cheese. If you aren't sure if your yogurt is active, you can add the contents of a probiotic capsule to your mixture before leaving it out to ferment.

MACADAMIA RICOTTA

Makes: 2 cups • Prep time: 10 minutes • Total time: 1-2 days

2 cup macadamia nuts, soaked   Contents of 1 probiotic capsule

½ tsp salt

Place macadamia nuts in a bowl, cover with water, and let soak for at least 8 hours. Drain and use immediately, or store in a sealed container in the refrigerator until ready to use.

In a high-power blender,* combine soaked macadamia nuts and salt. Blend on high until smooth and fluffy, adding a splash of water only if necessary (you may have to use the tamper tool). Add the probiotic and blend on low to incorporate.

Pour mixture into a bowl, cover loosely with a clean towel, and let sit at room temperature for one to two days.

Store in a sealed container in the refrigerator for up to two weeks.

*If you do not have a high-power blender, you can use a food processor. Just note that it may take a little longer and the final product will not be quite as smooth.

BRAZIL NUT PARMESAN

Makes: 2 cups • Prep time: 5 minutes • Total time: 5 minutes

1 ½ cup Brazil nuts*

⅓ cup nutritional yeast

1 tsp garlic powder

½ tsp salt

In a food processor, process all ingredients into a fine crumb.

Brazil nut parm is a great addition to most recipes. Use it as a garnish on zucchini noodles, caulifower crust pizza, and salads!

Store in a sealed container in the refrigerator for up to one month.

*You can use cashews in place of brazil nuts, or a combination of the two. Be sure that the nuts you use are dry (moisture will affect the texture of the final product).

NACHO CHEESE

½ cup sunflower seeds

½ cup Brazil nuts

½ cup water

¼ cup red bell pepper

2 Tbsp nutritional yeast

2 Tbsp lemon juice

1 tsp chickpea miso

1 clove garlic

½ tsp salt

¼ tsp turmeric

In a blender, combine all ingredients and blend on high until smooth (you may have to use the tamper tool). Taste and adjust flavors according to your preference.

Use this cheese in our nacho recipe (page 72), or serve over taco salad!

Store in a sealed container in the refrigerator for up to one week.

FRESH SALSA

2 cups tomato, seeded and diced

¼ cup red onion, finely chopped

¼ cup cilantro, minced

1 clove garlic, minced

¼ tsp salt

Pinch of black pepper

Combine all ingredients in a bowl. Taste and adjust the flavors according to your preference. For extra flavor, try adding some diced jalapeno or a squeeze of lime!

Serve with tortilla chips, chiles rellenos, or taco salad.

Store in a sealed container in the refrigerator for up to three days.

GUACAMOLE

Makes: 2 cups • Prep time: 15 minutes • Total time: 15 minutes

4 medium avocados

¼ cup red onion, minced

1 small tomato, seeded and diced

2 Tbsp cilantro, minced (optional)

2-3 Tbsp lime juice

¼-½ tsp salt

In a bowl, mash avocados with a fork or potato masher.* Add the remaining ingredients and stir to combine. Taste and adjust the flavors according to your preference.

To store, sprinkle the top with lime juice, seal with plastic wrap, and keep in the refrigerator for up to two days.

*For smooth and velvety guacamole, process the avocado in a food processor.

MEXICAN "BEAN" DIP

Makes: 2 cups • Prep time: 15 minutes • Total time: 15 minutes

⅓ cup sundried tomatoes, soaked

4 medium avocados

¼ cup red onion, diced

2 Tbsp lime juice

1 Tbsp chili powder

1 tsp cumin

1 clove garlic, minced

½ tsp salt

Place sundried tomatoes in a blender or food processor and grind into small pieces. Add all remaining ingredients and blend until mostly smooth. Taste and adjust the flavors according to your preference.

Serve this dip with raw tortilla chips, or add it to tacos and tostadas.

To store, sprinkle the top with lime juice, seal with plastic wrap, and keep in the refrigerator for up to two days.

ALMOND HUMMUS

1 large zucchini, peeled
⅔ cup almonds
⅓ cup raw tahini

¼ cup lemon juice
½ tsp garlic powder
¼ tsp salt

Place all ingredients in a blender and blend on high until smooth, adding a splash of water if necessary. Taste and adjust flavors according to your preference.

Top with a drizzle of olive oil and some chopped parsley, or mix in your favorite herbs and spices. Serve with sliced veggies or flackers.

Store in a sealed container in the refrigerator for up to one week.

SPROUTED HUMMUS

Makes: 2 cups • Prep time: 20 minutes • Total time: 3-5 days

Basic Recipe:

1 cup dried chickpeas

3 cups filtered water

½ cup raw tahini

¼ cup lemon juice

2 Tbsp olive oil

½ tsp salt

Sundried tomato and basil:

½ cup basil, finely chopped

¼ cup sundried tomato, chopped

Dash of black pepper

Jalapeno-cilantro:

1 small jalapeno, minced

½ cup fresh cilantro, chopped

Dash of cumin

Garlic:

2 cloves garlic, minced or pressed

Red pepper:

1 small red bell pepper, diced

Place chickpeas and water in a bowl and let soak for 16-18 hours. Using a colander, a straining bag, or a jar with a sprouting lid, drain and rinse. Let sit at room temperature for 2-4 days, rinsing twice a day until they sprout ¼- to ½-inch tails.

Place all the ingredients for the basic recipe in a high-power blender and blend on high until smooth, adding a splash of water if necessary. Fold or blend in any additional ingredients you are using.

Store in a sealed container in the refrigerator for up to one week.

OLIVE TAPENADE

Makes: 1.5 cups • Prep time: 15 minutes • Total time: 15 minutes

½ cup Brazil nuts or pine nuts

1 cup kalamata olives

3 Tbsp capers

3 Tbsp parsley, chopped

3 Tbsp olive oil

2 Tbsp lemon juice

2 cloves garlic, minced

Pinch of black pepper

In a food processor, process nuts until they form crumbs. Add remaining ingredients and pulse into fine pieces (not too much, or it will turn into a paste). Taste and adjust flavors according to your preference.

Serve with flackers or nut bread, or mix with chopped tomatoes and basil and serve over zoodles.

Store in a sealed container in the refrigerator for up to two weeks.

MAIN DISHES

Veggie Burgers	59		Zoodles with Marinara	81
Mushroom Burgers	60		Broccoli Manicotti	83
Jalapeño Burgers	61		Cauliflower Alfredo	84
Nutty Joes	62		Avocado Pesto	86
Philly Cheese Steak	63		Walnut Pesto	87
Neptune Salad	64		Cauliflower Pizza	89
Eggless Salad	66		Lasagna	91
Chickenless Salad	67		Falafel	93
Mac-n-Cheese	69		Veggie Wrap	94
Tacos	70		Nori Rolls	96
Nachos	72		Spring Rolls	97
Enchiladas	75		Vegetable Stir Fry	99
Stuffed Tomatoes	77		Tempeh Fried Rice	101
Chiles Rellenos	78		Almond Pad Thai	102
Stuffed Mushrooms	80		Curried Vegetables	104

VEGGIE BURGERS

Makes: 8 burgers • Prep time: 40 minutes • Total time: 22-24 hours

2 cup mushrooms	½ cup cilantro or parsley, chopped
1 cup walnuts	¼ cup tamari
1 cup sunflower seeds	3 Tbsp flax seed, ground
1 cup pumpkin seeds	1 Tbsp dried oregano
1 medium zucchini	1 Tbsp cumin
1 medium carrot	2 cloves garlic, minced
2 ribs celery	½ tsp ground mustard seed
½ cup yellow onion	½ tsp salt

Place the mushrooms in a saucepan and cover with water. Bring to a boil, then reduce to a simmer and let cook for 5 minutes. Drain and let cool.

In a food processor, combine walnuts, pumpkin seeds, and sunflower seeds. Process into a coarse flour, then pour into a large bowl and set aside. Place the mushrooms, celery, onion, and cilantro/parsley in the food processor and pulse until finely chopped. Add to the bowl of ground nuts and seeds.

Shred zucchini and carrot into the mixture. Add all remaining ingredients and stir to combine. Shape ½-cup portions into patties and place on a Teflex sheet.

Dehydrate at 105 °F for 4 hours, then flip onto a mesh tray and continue dehydrating for 16-18 hours.

Store in a sealed container in the refrigerator for up to four days.

MUSHROOM BURGERS

Makes: 6 burgers • Prep time: 30 minutes • Total time: 20-22 hours

3 cups mushrooms

1 cup walnuts or pecans

¾ cup sunflower seeds

2 ribs celery, chopped

½ cup onion, chopped

¼ cup tamari

2 Tbsp nutritional yeast

1 Tbsp chickpea miso

1 Tbsp olive oil

1 clove garlic

Place the mushrooms in a saucepan and cover with water. Bring to a boil, then reduce to a simmer and let cook for 5 minutes. Drain and let cool.

Place all ingredients in food processor and process until the mixture is mostly smooth with some texture remaining.

Shape ½-cup portions into patties and place on a Teflex sheet.

Dehydrate at 105 °F for 4 hours, then flip onto a mesh tray and continue dehydrating for 16-18 hours.

Store in a sealed container in the refrigerator for up to four days.

JALAPEÑO BURGERS

Makes: 6 burgers • Prep time: 20 minutes • Total time: 18-22 hours

2 cups walnuts

1 cup sunflower seeds

3 jalapeños, seeded and chopped

½ cup cilantro, chopped

½ cup yellow onion, chopped

¼ cup coconut aminos

2 Tbsp sundried tomatoes

1 Tbsp chickpea miso

1 Tbsp nutritional yeast

1 Tbsp flax seed, ground

1 clove garlic

¼ tsp smoked paprika (optional)

Place all ingredients in a food processor and process until it is mostly smooth with some texture remaining, adding a splash of water if necessary.

Shape ½-cup portions into patties and place on a mesh dehydrator tray.

Dehydrate at 105 °F for 18-22 hours.

Store in a sealed container in the refrigerator for up to four days.

NUTTY JOES

Makes: 4 servings • Prep time: 20 minutes • Total time: 20 minutes

1 ½ cup walnuts

2 tomatoes, seeded and chopped

¼ cup sun-dried tomatoes, soaked

½ red bell pepper, chopped

2 Tbsp olive oil

2 cloves garlic

1 Tbsp chili powder

1 tsp dried oregano

½ tsp cumin

½ tsp salt

¼ tsp black pepper

Place walnuts in food processor and pulse to crumble texture. Pour into a bowl and set aside.

Add remaining ingredients to the food processor and blend until mostly smooth. Taste and adjust the flavors according to your preference. Pour the sauce over the walnuts and stir to combine.

Serve on a cabbage leaf and garnish with sprouts if desired.

Store in a sealed container in the refrigerator for up to three days.

PHILLY CHEESE STEAK

For the steak:

4 portobello mushrooms, sliced

¼ cup avocado oil

¼ cup tamari

1 tsp cumin

1 tsp apple cider vinegar

For the vegetables:

2 green bell peppers, sliced

1 white onion, sliced

2 Tbsp avocado oil

1 Tbsp coconut aminos

1 clove garlic, minced

¼ tsp black pepper

For the cheese:

¾ cup sunflower seeds

¼ cup pine nuts

½ cup water

2 Tbsp lemon juice

1 tsp onion powder

¼ tsp salt

Place all the steak ingredients in a bowl, toss to combine, and place in the refrigerator overnight to marinate.

Place all vegetable ingredients in a bowl, toss to combine, and place in the dehydrator at 105 °F for 8-12 hours, until they have a cooked texture.

Place all cheese ingredients in a blender and blend until creamy.

When you're ready to serve, cook the mushrooms over medium heat for 5-10 minutes. To serve, layer ingredients in a romaine leaf or over a bed of lettuce.

NEPTUNE SALAD

Makes: 4 servings • Prep time: 20 minutes • Total time: 20 minutes

For the mayonnaise:

½ cup cashews	1 Tbsp avocado oil
¾ cup water	1 clove garlic
3 Tbsp lemon juice	½ tsp salt

For the base:

1 ½ cup sunflower seeds	¼ cup red onion, minced
1 cup almonds	¼ cup parsley, minced
1-2 ribs celery, diced	¼ cup dill relish

Place the mayonnaise ingredients in a blender and blend on high until smooth.

In a food processor, combine sunflower seeds, almonds, and mayonnaise. Process until it reaches a texture that resembles tuna salad.

Pour mixture into a bowl and stir in celery, red onion, parsley, and dill relish. Taste and adjust the flavors according to your preference. Add some crushed nori or dulse flakes for a seafood flavor.

Serve over a bed of lettuce and top with chopped tomatoes and sprouts, if desired.

Store in a sealed container in the refrigerator for up to one week.

EGGLESS SALAD

Makes: 4 servings • Prep time: 20 minutes • Total time: 20 minutes

For the sauce:

1 ½ cups cashews	1 clove garlic
½ cup water	½ tsp turmeric
2 Tbsp lemon juice	¼ tsp black salt (optional)
1 Tbsp chickpea miso	¼ tsp black pepper

For the base:

3 ribs celery, diced	½ small red onion, diced
1 yellow bell pepper, diced	1 avocado, diced

Place the sauce ingredients in a high-power blender and blend on high until smooth (this is a very thick sauce, so you may have to use your blender's tamper tool).

In a bowl, combine celery, yellow bell pepper, onion, and avocado. Stir in the sauce. Taste and adjust the flavors according to your preference.

Top with parsley, chives, and black pepper if desired.

Store in a sealed container in the refrigerator for up to two days.

CHICKENLESS SALAD

Makes: 4 servings • Prep time: 20 minutes • Total time: 20 minutes

For the mayonnaise:

¾ cup cashews

½ cup water

2 Tbsp dijon mustard

2 Tbsp coconut aminos

1 Tbsp chickpea miso

1 clove garlic

For the base:

8 oz package tempeh, diced

½ cup walnuts

1 rib celery, diced

¼ small red onion, diced

¼ cup parsley, minced (optional)

Place the mayonnaise ingredients in a blender and blend on high until smooth.

In a food processor, combine tempeh, walnuts, and mayonnaise. Pulse a few times, until the mixture reaches a texture that resembles chicken salad.

Pour mixture into a bowl and stir in remaining ingredients. Taste and adjust the flavors according to your preference.

Serve on a cabbage leaf or over a bed of lettuce. Top with shredded carrot and smoked paprika if desired.

Store in a sealed container in the refrigerator for up to four days.

MAC-N-CHEESE

Makes: 6 servings • Prep time: 30 minutes • Total time: 2 hours

For the macaroni:

8 yellow squash, spiralized   Pinch of salt

For the cheese:

1 ½ cup cashews   1 clove garlic

½ cup water   ½ tsp onion powder

¼ cup nutritional yeast   ½ tsp turmeric

1 Tbsp lemon juice   ½ tsp salt

Roughly chop the spiralized squash, toss with a pinch of salt, and let sit in a colander for 15 to 20 minutes to soften.

In a high-power blender, combine cheese ingredients and blend on high until completely smooth (this is a very thick sauce, so you may have to use your blender's tamper tool).

Mix spiralized squash and cheese sauce in a bowl and then spread into a glass dish.

Place in the dehydrator at 110 °F for 1 to 2 hours to warm through.

Top with Brazil nut parmesan and a pinch of black pepper or smoked paprika.

Store in a sealed container in the refrigerator for up to two days.

TACOS

Makes: 6 servings • Prep time: 45 minutes • Total time: 16-18 hours

For the tortillas:

2 cups corn, fresh or frozen

1 cup cauliflower, chopped

½ cup onion

¼ cup flax seed, ground

1-2 Tbsp nutritional yeast (optional)

1 clove garlic

1 tsp salt

½ tsp black pepper

For the taco meat:

2 cups walnuts

3 Tbsp tamari

1 Tbsp cumin

1 tsp dried Mexican oregano

1 tsp garlic powder

½ tsp black pepper

For the fixings (optional):

Mexican "beans" (page 52)

Guacamole (page 51)

Fresh salsa (page 49)

Cilantro and green onions

Place all tortilla ingredients in a food processor and process until mostly smooth. Scoop ⅓-cup portions onto Teflex sheets and spread into 5-inch circles between ⅛- and ¼-inch thick. Dehydrate at 115 °F for 16-18 hours, until dry but pliable. Or dehydrate until crispy to make tostadas!

Place all taco meat ingredients in the food processor and pulse until the texture becomes crumbly. Taste and adjust the flavors according to your preference.

Assemble your tacos with the fixings of your choice.

NACHOS

Makes: 6 servings • Prep time: 1 hour • Total time: 22-24 hours

For the tortilla chips:

2 cups corn, fresh or frozen	1-2 Tbsp nutritional yeast (optional)
1 cup cauliflower, chopped	1 clove garlic
½ cup onion	1 tsp salt
¼ cup flax seed, ground	½ tsp black pepper

For the nacho meat:

1 cup sunflower seeds	1 green onion
1 cup walnuts	1 clove garlic
¼ cup cilantro	2 tsp cumin
3 Tbsp lime juice	1 tsp chili powder
1 jalapeno, seeded (optional)	½ tsp salt

For the nacho cheese:

½ cup sunflower seeds	2 Tbsp lemon juice
½ cup Brazil nuts	1 tsp chickpea miso
½ cup water	1 clove garlic
¼ cup red bell pepper	½ tsp salt
2 Tbsp nutritional yeast	¼ tsp turmeric

For the fixings:

Chopped tomatoes	Sliced green onions
Diced avocado	Chopped cilantro

For the tortilla chips, place all ingredients in a food processor and process until mostly smooth. Scoop ⅓-cup portions onto Teflex sheets and spread into 5-inch circles between ⅛- and ¼-inch thick.

Dehydrate at 115 °F for 22-24 hours, or until crispy. Cut each tortilla into 6 triangular sections to create chips (this can be done before or after they are fully dehydrated).

For the nacho meat, place all ingredients in a food processor and process until crumbly, adding a splash of water if necessary. Taste and adjust the flavors according to your preference.

For the nacho cheese, place all ingredients in a blender and blend on high until smooth (you may have to use the tamper tool). Taste and adjust the flavors according to your preference.

To assemble, spread the tortilla chips on a serving platter and top with nacho meat, nacho cheese, and any fixings of your choice. Serve immediately.

ENCHILADAS

Makes: 6 servings · Prep time: 1 hour · Total time: 12-14 hours

For the tortillas:

2 cups corn, fresh or frozen	1-2 Tbsp nutritional yeast (optional)
1 cup tomato, seeded and chopped	1 clove garlic
⅓ cup onion	1 tsp salt
¼ cup flax seed, ground	½ tsp black pepper

For the filling:

1 cup sunflower or pumpkin seeds	1 tsp chili powder
1 cup walnuts	1 tsp cumin
1 jalapeno, minced	½ tsp dried Mexican oregano
½ cup cilantro, chopped	1 clove garlic, minced
¼ cup red onion, diced	¼ tsp black pepper
3 Tbsp tamari	

For the enchilada sauce:

1 cup tomatoes, seeded and chopped	½ tsp onion powder
½ cup sundried tomatoes	¼ tsp garlic powder
2 Tbsp coconut aminos	¼ tsp salt
2 tsp chili powder	

For the tortilla chips, place all ingredients in a food processor and process until mostly smooth. Scoop ⅓-cup portions onto Teflex sheets and spread into 5-inch circles between ⅛- and ¼-inch thick. Dehydrate at 105 °F for 12-14 hours, until dry but still pliable. If they get too dry, dip each one in water and return to the dehydrator for about 20 minutes.

For the filling, place all ingredients in a food processor and pulse into a crumbly texture. Taste and adjust flavors according to your preference. Set aside.

For the sauce, place all ingredients in a blender and blend until smooth. Taste and adjust flavors according to your preference.

To assemble the enchiladas, divide filling among the tortillas, roll each one, and place on your serving dish seam-side down. Spoon the sauce over the top.

Serve with avocado, cilantro, lime, and coconut-cashew "sour-cream."

STUFFED TOMATOES

Makes: 4 servings • Prep time: 30 minutes • Total time: 30 minutes

8 large tomatoes, whole

2 cups corn

2 avocados, diced

½ cup cilantro, chopped

2 cups tomato, chopped

¼ cup sundried tomato

¼ cup red onion

1 Tbsp chili powder

2 Tbsp lime juice

1 tsp salt

Carve a hole in the top of each whole tomato and hollow out the inside.

In a bowl, mix together corn, avocado, and cilantro.

In a food processor combine chopped tomato, sun dried tomato, red onion, chili powder, lime juice, and salt. Pour over corn mixture and stir to combine. Let sit for 10-15 minutes.

Fill hollowed tomatoes with the corn mixture and serve.

CHILES RELLENOS

Makes: 4 servings • Prep time: 30 minutes • Total time: 22-24 hours

2 Anaheim or Poblano peppers

1 cup sunflower seeds

½ red bell pepper

¼ cup water

2 Tbsp lemon juice

1 Tbsp chickpea miso

1 clove garlic

½ tsp salt

2 Tbsp nutritional yeast

Slice the chiles in half lengthwise and remove the seeds, veins, and stem. Rub the outside of the peppers with a little olive oil to prevent the skin from getting too dry in the dehydrator.

In a food processor, combine all ingredients except chiles and nutritional yeast. Process until mostly smooth.

Fill the chiles with the mixture and sprinkle with nutritional yeast. Place on a Teflex sheet and dehydrate at 105 °F for 22-24 hours, until the peppers are soft.

Serve with fresh salsa or chimichurri sauce.

Store in a sealed container in the refrigerator for up to two days.

STUFFED MUSHROOMS

For the marinated mushrooms:

4 portobello mushrooms

2 Tbsp olive oil

1 Tbsp coconut aminos

1 Tbsp balsamic vinegar

1 clove garlic, minced

¼ tsp black pepper

For the filling:

1 tomato, seeded

1 cup pecans

½ cup sunflower seeds

2 ribs celery, chopped

1 medium carrot, shredded

¼ cup parsley, chopped

2 Tbsp red onion, diced

2 tsp Italian seasoning

½ tsp salt

¼ tsp garlic powder

In a small bowl, whisk together marinade ingredients. Place mushrooms in a large bowl and pour marinade over them, tossing gently to coat. Let sit for 1 hour.

To make the filling, place the tomato in a food processor and blend until liquified. Add the pecans and sunflower seeds, pulse into pieces. Add remaining ingredients and pulse to combine (do not process into a paste). Spread this mixture onto a Teflex sheet and place in the dehydrator at 110 °F while you cook the mushrooms.

Heat a pan over medium heat. Cook each mushroom for about five minutes on one side, then flip and cook for 3 more minutes, or until tender.

Portion the filling into the mushrooms and top with Brazil nut parmesan, if desired.

ZOODLES WITH MARINARA AND NUTBALLS

Makes: 4 servings • Prep time: 45 minutes • Total time: 18-20 hours

For the nutballs:

1 cup walnuts	1 Tbsp tamari
½ cup sunflower seeds	1 Tbsp dried parsley
½ cup zucchini	2 tsp dried oregano
¼ cup red or yellow onion	1 clove garlic, minced
¼ cup flax seed, ground	½ tsp salt

For the marinara:

3 cups tomatoes, seeded	2 Tbsp fresh basil, chopped
¼ cup sundried tomatoes	2 tsp fresh oregano, chopped
2 Tbsp olive oil	¼ tsp salt
1 clove garlic	

For the zoodles:

6 medium zucchini, spiralized	Pinch of salt

For the nutballs, place all ingredients in a food processor and process until the mixture is finely ground, adding a splash of water if necessary. Form mixture into balls and place on a mesh dehydrator sheet. Dehydrate at 105 °F for 18-20 hours.

For the marinara, place all ingredients, except herbs, in a blender and blend until smooth. Add the herbs and blend on low to combine.

Toss the spiralized zucchini with a pinch of salt and let sit in a colander for 15-20 minutes. Top with marinara and nutballs.

BROCCOLI MANICOTTI

Makes: 6 servings • Prep time: 1 hour • Total time: 1 hour

For the shells:

3 large zucchini	Pinch of salt

For the filling:

4 cups broccoli florets	3 Tbsp nutritional yeast
½ cup red onion, chopped	3 Tbsp lemon juice
1 ½ cups macadamia nuts	1 tsp garlic powder
¾ cup water	½-1 tsp salt

For the sauce:

2 cups tomatoes	1 Tbsp olive oil
¼ cup sundried tomatoes	1 clove garlic
1 Tbsp Italian seasoning	¼ tsp salt

For the shells, use a mandolin to shave thin strips of zucchini. Toss with a pinch of salt and let sit in a colander while you prepare the filling and sauce.

For the filling, place the broccoli and red onion in a food processor and pulse until finely chopped. Pour into a bowl and set aside. Place all remaining ingredients in the food processor and process until smooth. Taste and adjust the flavors, then pour the mixture over the broccoli and stir to combine.

For the sauce, place all ingredients in a blender and blend until mostly smooth.

To assemble, place three zucchini strips side by side, overlapping them slightly. Place a few spoonfuls of filling at one end, roll it up, and top with sauce.

CAULIFLOWER ALFREDO

1 medium head of cauliflower	½ tsp chickpea miso
1 ¼ cup cashews	1 clove garlic
¾ cup water	½ tsp salt
2 Tbsp lemon juice	Pinch of black pepper

Chop the florets of the cauliflower into pea-sized pieces, place in a bowl, and set aside while you prepare the alfredo sauce.

In a high-power blender, combine all remaining ingredients and blend on high until velvety smooth. Taste and adjust the flavors according to your preference.

Pour the sauce over the cauliflower, stir, and let sit at room temperature or in the dehydrator for 20-30 minutes to soften.

Serve with fresh parsley, if desired.

Store in a sealed container in the refrigerator for up to two days.

ZOODLES WITH AVOCADO PESTO

Makes: 4 servings • Prep time: 30 minutes • Total time: 30 minutes

For the zoodles:

6 medium zucchini, spiralized

Pinch of salt

For the avocado pesto:

2 small avocados

2 cups basil, chopped

1 Tbsp lemon juice

1 Tbsp olive oil

1 clove garlic

½ tsp salt

Toss spiralized zucchini with a pinch of salt and let sit in a colander while you prepare the sauce.

In a food processor, combine all ingredients for the avocado pesto and process until smooth.

In a bowl, mix the zoodles with avocado pesto and top with cherry tomatoes, if desired. Serve immediately.

CAULIFLOWER WITH WALNUT PESTO

Makes: 4 servings • Prep time: 30 minutes • Total time: 30 minutes

1 medium head of cauliflower

½ cup walnuts

4 cups basil

2 cloves garlic

2 Tbsp nutritional yeast

1 Tbsp lemon juice

⅓ cup olive oil

½ tsp salt

Chop the florets of the cauliflower into pea-sized pieces, toss with a pinch of salt, and place in the dehydrator or let sit at room temperature while you prepare the pesto.

In a food processor, grind walnuts until they begin to form a thick nut butter. Add basil, garlic, nutritional yeast, and lemon juice and process until basil is finely chopped. Add olive oil and salt, process to combine.

Pour the pesto over the cauliflower and toss to coat. Top with cherry tomatoes if desired. Serve immediately.

CAULIFLOWER CRUST PIZZA

Makes: 12" pizza • Prep time: 45 minutes • Total time: 18-20 hours

For the crust:

1 ½ cups almonds	1 tsp onion powder
3 cups cauliflower, chopped	1 tsp garlic powder
¼ cup flax seed, ground	1 tsp salt

For the sauce:

1 cup tomatoes, chopped	1 clove garlic
¼ cup sun-dried tomatoes	¼ tsp sea salt
1 Tbsp olive oil	2 tsp fresh oregano, chopped

For the toppings:

1 cup seasonal veggies, chopped	¼ cup Brazil nut parmesan (page 46)
½ cup macadamia ricotta (page 45)	2 Tbsp basil, chopped

For the crust, place almonds in a food processor and grind into a flour. Add all remaining ingredients and process into a thick, slightly grainy dough. Pour dough onto a Teflex sheet and spread into a 12-inch circle. Dehydrate at 110 °F for 18-22 hours, flipping onto a mesh tray after the first few hours.

For the sauce, combine all ingredients except oregano in a blender and blend on high until smooth. Stir in the oregano. Taste and adjust the flavors as needed.

Spread sauce onto the cauliflower crust and top with any toppings of your choice. Enjoy immediately or place back in the dehydrator for another 1-2 hours.

LASAGNA

For the zoodles:

6-8 medium zucchini   Pinch of salt

For the sauce:

2 cups tomatoes, seeded   1 clove garlic

⅓ cup sundried tomatoes   ¼ tsp salt

1 Tbsp olive oil   2 tsp fresh oregano, chopped

For the cheese*:

¾ cups cashews, soaked   2 Tbsp lemon juice

¾ cup macadamia nuts, soaked   ½ tsp salt

3 Tbsp nutritional yeast

For the pesto:

⅓ cup pine nuts or walnuts   1 clove garlic

4 cups basil   ½ tsp salt

2 Tbsp nutritional yeast   ½ cup olive oil

1 Tbsp lemon juice

To make the zoodles, use a mandoline to slice each zucchini lengthwise into thin strips (about ⅓-inch thick). Place them in a colander, toss with a pinch of salt and let sit for at least 20 minutes, until pliable.

For the cheese, place all ingredients in a blender and blend on high until smooth, adding a splash of water if necessary (you may need to use the tamper tool). Alternatively, this can be done in a food processor, but it may take a little longer and the texture will be more grainy.

For the sauce, place all ingredients, except oregano, in a blender and blend until mostly smooth. Stir in the oregano. Taste and adjust the flavors according to your preference.

For the pesto, place the nuts in a food processor and grind them until they begin to form a thick nut butter. Add basil, garlic, nutritional yeast, lemon juice, and salt; process until the basil is finely chopped. Add olive oil and pulse to combine.

To assemble, place a layer of zoodles on the bottom of a small, square baking dish (about 8" x 8"). Spread a little sauce over them, then top with dollops of nut cheese and pesto. Continue layering the zoodles, sauce, cheese, and pesto until you run out.

Top the final layer of zoodles with some sauce and Brazil nut parmesan, if desired. Serve immediately.

*For a fermented cheese, prepare it the day before. Omit the lemon juice and stir in the contents of one probiotic capsule after blending. Cover and let sit at room temperature overnight.

FALAFEL

Makes: 4 servings • Prep time: 20 minutes • Total time: 16-18 hours

For the veggies:

1 cup zucchini, chopped	½ cup parsley (or more, if desired)
¾ cup sunflower seeds	¼ cup tamari or coconut aminos
¾ cup almonds	2 tsp curry powder
¼ cup carrot, chopped	1 tsp cumin
¼ cup red or yellow onion	1 clove garlic

Combine all ingredients in a food processor and process until the mixture forms a grainy dough. Taste and adjust the flavors according to your preference, keeping in mind that the flavors will lose intensity in the dehydrator.

Using a cookie dough scooper or a tablespoon, scoop portions onto a mesh dehydrator sheet and shape them into slightly flattened balls. Dehydrate at 105 °F for 16-18 hours, until crispy on the outside and soft on the inside.

Serve on a bed of greens with tomatoes, olives, and cucumber. Top with hummus or lemon-tahini dressing and sprouts.

VEGGIE WRAP

Makes: 6 servings • Prep time: 45 minutes • Total time: 16-18 hours

For the wrap:

½ cup young Thai coconut meat	1 cups water
¾ cup flax seeds	1 clove garlic
¼ cup sundried tomatoes	1 tsp salt
2 cup tomatoes, chopped	¼ cup fresh basil, chopped

For the filling:

1 small cucumber, sliced	1 small avocado, sliced
1 red bell pepper, sliced	¼ small red onion, sliced
1 carrot, shredded	Broccoli sprouts or lettuce
1 tomato, diced	Hummus or nut cheese

In a high-power blender, blend all ingredients except basil until smooth (this mixture is very thick, so you may have to use your blender's tamper tool). Transfer to a bowl and fold in basil.

Scoop ½-cup portions onto Teflex sheets, spreading into 7 to 8 inch circles, between ⅛- and ¼-inch thick. Dehydrate at 105 °F for 16-18 hours, or until dry but pliable.

If they get crispy, dip in water and place back in the dehydrator for 20 minutes.

Fill the wraps with the veggies of your choice! Feel free to change the recipe by using seasonal, local vegetables. Also, play around with the flavors by adding your favorite dressings and sauces.

NORI ROLLS

Makes: 4 servings • Prep time: 45 minutes • Total time: 45 minutes

For the nori rolls:

4 sheets nori seaweed	½ cup shredded carrot
3 cups cauliflower, riced	½ red bell pepper, thinly sliced
1 large avocado, thinly sliced	½ cucumber, sliced lengthwise
1-2 cups sprouts or microgreens	2 green onions, sliced lengthwise

For the dipping sauce:

⅓ cup tamari	2 tsp toasted sesame oil
1 Tbsp unsalted tahini	2 tsp fresh ginger, minced

Lay one sheet of nori on a sushi mat, shiny side down. Spread a layer of cauliflower rice over the nori, leaving at least one inch uncovered at the far edge. Layer on the avocado, sprouts, carrots, red bell pepper, cucumber, and green onion.

To roll, start at the close edge by griping the nori sheet and the sushi mat together, and folding the edge over the filling. Roll the nori away from you, squeezing with the mat as you go to help keep it taut. Just before completing the roll, dip your finger in water and run it along the far edge of the nori sheet. This will seal the seam of the wrap. Let the nori roll sit seam-side down for a minute or so before cutting. Repeat this process for the remaining rolls.

Cut the nori rolls in half or into bite-size rounds. Whisk together the ingredients for the dipping sauce, and serve.

SPRING ROLLS

For the spring rolls:

4 sheets brown rice paper

1 cup sprouts or microgreens

½ cup cilantro, chopped

¼ purple cabbage, shredded

1 cucumber, shredded

1 carrot, shredded

1 red bell pepper, chopped small

1 avocado, diced

For the sauce:

½ cup almond butter

⅓ cup water

3 Tbsp tamari or coconut aminos

1 Tbsp ginger, minced

Place the sprouts, cilantro, and vegetables in a large bowl and toss together.

In a small bowl, whisk together all ingredients for the sauce. Pour the sauce over the veggies and toss to combine, or keep the sauce separate and serve for dipping.

To assemble the spring rolls, dip a sheet of rice paper in filtered water for about 5-10 seconds, then lay it on a clean surface and place a pile of vegetables in the center of the sheet. Grip the edge of the rice paper that is closest to you and fold it over the veggies. Fold in the sides, and continue rolling away from you, making it as tight as possible. Repeat this process for the remaining rolls.

VEGETABLE STIR FRY

Makes: 4 servings • Prep time: 1 hour • Total time: 1 hour

For the rice:

½ cup almonds

1 medium head cauliflower

2 Tbsp coconut aminos

1 Tbsp fresh ginger

For the vegetables:

8 shiitake mushrooms, sliced

1 head broccoli, chopped

1 small carrot, thinly sliced

1 red bell pepper, sliced

½ cup purple cabbage, thinly sliced

2 green onions, thinly sliced

For the sauce:

¼ cup tamari

2 Tbsp coconut oil, melted

1 Tbsp toasted sesame oil

2 tsp fresh ginger, minced

1 clove of garlic, minced

To make the rice, place the almonds in a food processor and grind into a flour. Add the remaining ingredients and pulse until it begins to resemble rice (this may need to be done in two or three batches). Spread the rice onto a Teflex sheet and dehydrate at 115 °F while you prepare the veggies.

In a frying pan, cook the sliced shiitake mushrooms for 5-7 minutes over medium heat, adding a splash of water to keep them from sticking. Remove from heat and let cool. Combine with all remaining veggies in a bowl.

In a small bowl, whisk together the sauce ingredients. Taste and adjust the flavors. Pour the sauce over the veggies and toss to combine. Serve over cauliflower rice.

TEMPEH FRIED RICE

Makes: 4 servings • Prep time: 30 minutes • Total time: 2 hours

For the tempeh:

1 package tempeh, diced	1 clove garlic, minced
3 Tbsp tamari	½ tsp onion powder
1 Tbsp toasted sesame oil	

For the vegetables:

½ cup green peas	1 Tbsp coconut aminos
½ cup carrots, diced	

For the rice:

½ cup almonds	2-3 Tbsp tamari
1 medium head cauliflower	1-2 Tbsp fresh ginger, minced
2 Tbsp coconut or avocado oil	

For the tempeh, place all ingredients in a bowl and toss to combine. Repeat this process for the vegetables. Cover both bowls and let marinate at room temperature for about one hour, or in the refrigerator overnight.

For the rice, place almonds in a food processor and grind into a flour. Add the remaining ingredients and pulse until it begins to resemble rice (this may need to be done in two or three batches).

Mix the tempeh and veggies into the cauliflower rice (leaving behind any extra liquid from the veggies). Enjoy immediately, or spread the mixture onto Teflex sheets and dehydrate at 115 °F for 1-2 hours, for a more "cooked" feel.

ALMOND PAD THAI

Makes: 4 servings • Prep time: 30 minutes • Total time: 30 minutes

For the sauce:

½ cup almond butter

¼ cup water

¼ cup tamari

1 Tbsp sesame oil

2 tsp lime juice

2 tsp fresh ginger, minced

1 clove garlic, minced

For the noodles and veggies:

16 oz of miracle or kelp noodles

1 large carrot, shredded

1 large red bell pepper, thinly sliced

1 cup purple cabbage, thinly sliced

1 cup microgreens

2 green onions, thinly sliced

In a small bowl, whisk together all sauce ingredients.

In a large bowl, combine the noodles, carrot, bell pepper and purple cabbage. Add the almond butter sauce and toss to coat.

Serve over microgreens and top with green onions.

Store in a sealed container in the refrigerator for up to two days.

CURRIED VEGETABLES

Makes: 4 servings • Prep time: 30 minutes • Total time: 30 minutes

For the sauce:

1 ½ cups coconut milk	2 tsp fresh ginger, minced
1 small tomato, seeded	1 clove garlic
1 Tbsp curry powder	½ tsp cumin
1 Tbsp coconut aminos	¼ tsp salt

For the vegetables:

4 cups cauliflower, chopped	½ cup purple cabbage, shredded
1 carrot, sliced	1 green onion, sliced
1 red bell pepper, sliced	

For the sauce, place all ingredients in a blender and blend until smooth. Taste and adjust the flavors according to your preference. Pour the sauce over the veggies and toss to combine.

Serve immediately or dehydrate at 115 for 1 to 2 hours to soften and warm. Top with cashew pieces and cilantro if desired.

SOUPS

Broccoli Soup	107
Chickenless Noodle Soup	108
Avocado Pea Soup	109
Cucumber Dill Soup	110
Smokey Corn soup	112
Mushroom Chili	113
Tomato Basil Soup	115
Butternut Squash Soup	116
Italian Mushroom Soup	117
Miso Soup	118
Coconut Curry	120

BROCCOLI SOUP

4 cups broccoli

1 large carrot

1 ½ cups warm water

⅓ cup cashews

¼ cup hemp seeds

2 Tbsp chickpea miso

1 Tbsp tamari

1 small clove garlic

1 tsp fresh ginger

Black pepper to taste

In a food processor, pulse broccoli until finely chopped. Place in a bowl and set aside. Add the carrot to the food processor and pulse until finely chopped. Mix it into the broccoli and set aside

In a blender, combine all remaining ingredients and blend until smooth. Pour this mixture over the broccoli and carrot. Taste and adjust the flavors according to your preference.

Serve with diced avocado and green onion, if desired.

Store in a sealed container in the refrigerator for up to two days.

CHICKENLESS NOODLE SOUP

Makes: 4 cups • Prep time: 20 minutes • Total time: 20 minutes

For te noodles:

1 zucchini, spiralized	Pinch of salt

For the soup:

2 ½ cups warm water	2 Tbsp cashew butter
2 ribs of celery	2 Tbsp coconut aminos
¼ cup carrot	1 Tbsp chickpea miso
¼ cup red onion	1 clove garlic
2 Tbsp mushroom powder*	¼ tsp salt
2 Tbsp fresh parsley	Black pepper to taste

Place spiralized zucchini in a colander and toss with a pinch of salt. Set aside to soften while you prepare the soup.

Combine all remaining ingredients in a blender and blend on high until smooth. Taste and adjust the flavors according to your preference. Mix the zoodles into the soup.

Serve with additional chopped parsley and a drizzle of olive oil, if desired.

*We recommend using a medicinal mushroom powder, such as turkey tail, reishi, chaga, or lion's mane.

AVOCADO PEA SOUP

Makes: 4 cups • Prep time: 10 minutes • Total time: 10 minutes

2 cups warm water

1 ½ cups green peas

½ cup spinach

2 Tbsp fresh parsley

1 small avocado

½ tsp salt

Place water, peas, spinach, and parsley in a blender and blend until smooth. Add avocado and salt, blend on low to combine.

Top with black pepper and serve immediately.

CUCUMBER DILL SOUP

2 cups cucumber, peeled and seeded

2 cups almond milk

½ cup coconut yogurt*

½ tsp salt

1 Tbsp fresh dill, minced

Black pepper to taste

In a blender, combine all ingredients except dill and blend until smooth. Stir in dill. Taste and adjust the flavors according to your preference.

Serve with a drizzle of olive oil.

*You can substitute the coconut yogurt with 1 Tbsp lemon juice, if necessary.

SMOKEY CORN SOUP

2 cups corn

1 yellow bell pepper

1 cup warm water

¾ cup coconut milk

¼ cup red onion, diced

¼-½ tsp smoked paprika

½ tsp salt

¼ tsp garlic powder

¼ tsp black pepper

¼ tsp cumin

Combine corn, bell pepper, water, and coconut milk in a blender and blend on high until smooth. Add the remaining ingredients and blend on low to combine. Taste and adjust the flavors according to your preference.

Serve with chopped tomato, diced avocado, and cilantro, if desired.

Store in a sealed container in the refrigerator for up to two days.

MUSHROOM CHILI

Makes: 4 cups • Prep time: 30 minutes • Total time: 30 minutes

1 cup cremini mushrooms

2 cups tomatoes, seeded and diced

2 cup walnuts or pecans

¼ cup corn (optional)

¼ cup sundried tomatoes, chopped

1 rib of celery, chopped

3 Tbsp tamari or coconut aminos

2 tsp chili powder

1 tsp onion powder

½ tsp garlic powder

½ tsp cumin

½ tsp paprika (sweet or smoked)

½ tsp salt

¼ tsp black pepper

Place mushrooms in a saucepan, cover with water, and bring to a boil. Reduce the heat and let simmer for 5 minutes. Drain the water and let the mushrooms cool.

Place all ingredients in a food processor and pulse until it reaches the consistency of chili. Taste and adjust the flavors according to your preference.

Serve with avocado, cilantro, and green onions.

Store in a sealed container in the refrigerator for up to two days.

TOMATO BASIL SOUP

Makes: 4 cups • Prep time: 15 minutes • Total time: 15 minutes

1 ¼ cup warm water

⅓ cup sundried tomatoes

¼ cup cashews*

1 clove garlic

3 cups tomatoes, seeded and diced

3 Tbsp fresh basil, minced

½ tsp salt

Black pepper to taste

In a high-power blender, combine the water, sundried tomatoes, cashews, and garlic. Blend on high until smooth. Add the diced tomatoes and blend until smooth (or pulse to retain some chunky texture, if desired).

Mix in the basil and black pepper. Serve with a drizzle of olive oil and some extra basil, if desired.

Store in a sealed container in the refrigerator for up to two days.

*If you do not have a high power blender, either soak the cashews before blending, or substitute with 1 Tbsp cashew butter.

BUTTERNUT SQUASH SOUP

Makes: 4 cups • Prep time: 15 minutes • Total time: 15 minutes

2 cups butternut squash, diced

2 cups warm water

½ cup cashews

1 rib of celery

1-2 tsp lemon juice

½ tsp salt

½ tsp dried sage

¼ tsp rosemary

Place all ingredients in a high-power blender and blend until smooth. Taste and adjust the flavors according to your preference.

Serve with a drizzle of olive oil or coconut cream. Top with black pepper and fresh parsley or basil, if desired.

Store in a sealed container in the refrigerator for up to two days.

ITALIAN MUSHROOM SOUP

Makes: 4 cups • Prep time: 30 minutes • Total time: 30 minutes

3 cups mushrooms

2 cups water

⅓ cup cashews

2 Tbsp sundried tomatoes

1 rib celery

1 slice of yellow onion

1 clove garlic

1 tsp chickpea miso

½ tsp Italian seasoning

¼ tsp salt

Place mushrooms in a saucepan, cover with water, and bring to a boil. Reduce the heat, cover, and let simmer for 5 minutes. Remove from heat, do not drain, and let cool.

Place cashews, sundried tomatoes, and mushrooms with water in a high-power blender and blend until smooth. Add remaining ingredients and blend again until smooth. Taste and adjust the flavors according to your preference.

Serve with parsley and brazil nut parmesan, if desired.

Store in a sealed container in the refrigerator for up to two days.

MISO SOUP

Makes: 4 cups • Prep time: 20 minutes • Total time: 20 minutes

3 cups warm water

1 cup mushrooms, chopped

½ cup cashews or hemp seeds

3 Tbsp chickpea miso

1 Tbsp tamari

1 Tbsp fresh ginger

1 small clove garlic

2 tsp sesame oil

¼ cup red pepper, thinly sliced

¼ cup purple cabbage, thinly sliced

¼ cup leek, thinly sliced

Place mushrooms in a saucepan, cover with water, and bring to a boil. Reduce the heat, cover, and let simmer for 5 minutes. Remove from heat, do not drain, and let cool.

Once cool, pour the contents of the saucepan into a blender, add all remaining ingredients except red pepper, cabbage, and leek. Blend until smooth. Alternatively, reserve half of the mushrooms to be mixed in at the end.

Add the vegetables and blend on low to combine.

Store in a sealed container in the refrigerator for up to two days.

COCONUT CURRY

2 red bell peppers

2 cups coconut milk

1 Tbsp coconut aminos

2 tsp yellow curry powder

1 tsp fresh ginger, minced

1 clove garlic

½ tsp salt

Black pepper to taste

Place all ingredients in a blender and blend until smooth. Taste and adjust the flavors according to your preference.

Serve with additional sliced red pepper or top with chopped cilantro, if desired.

Store in a sealed container in the refrigerator for up to two days.

SIDES

Sauerkraut	123
Cole Slaw	124
Root Salad	125
Thai Crunch Salad	126
Italian Sprout Salad	128
Avocado Kale Salad	129
Tabbouleh	131
Broccoli Salad	132
Fajitas	133
Hot Wings	135
Avocado Fries	136
Onion Rings	138

SAUERKRAUT

Makes: 1 quart • Prep time: 30 minutes • Total time: 7+ days

Basic recipe:

1 medium head of cabbage   1 Tbsp salt

Traditional:	Cilantro-jalapeno:
1 carrot, shredded	1 jalapeno, diced
1 tsp caraway seeds	½ cup cilantro, chopped

Garlic and dill:	Spicy ginger:
3 cloves garlic, chopped	2 Tbsp gincer, minced
2 Tbsp fresh dill (or 1 Tbsp dried)	2 tsp crushed red pepper

Chop or shred cabbage into small pieces, according to your preference. In a large bowl, toss with salt and let sit for 20 minutes. Massage the cabbage with your hands until it softens and releases enough liquid to cover itself.

Add any additional vegetables and seasoning you like!

Pack the cabbage into a jar and cover with the liquid. Place a weight on top of the cabbage to keep it submerged - this prevents it from becoming moldy.

Leave at room temperature for 7 or more days to ferment. Once it has reached your desired level of fermentation, cover tightly and store in the refrigerator.

COLE SLAW

For the slaw:

3 cups green cabbage, shredded

1 cup purple cabbage, shredded

1 cup carrot, shredded

For the dressing:

½ cup sunflower seeds

⅓ cup water

2 Tbsp apple cider vinegar

1 Tbsp lemon juice

1 Tbsp dijon mustard

½ Medjool date, pitted

½ tsp salt

¼ tsp celery seed

Black pepper to taste

In a large bowl, combine the cabbage and carrots. Set aside.

In a blender, combine all remaining ingredients except black pepper and blend until smooth. Taste and adjust flavors according to your preference.

Pour this mixture over the cabbage and carrots, and toss to combine. Season with black pepper.

Store in a sealed container in the refrigerator for up to two days.

ROOT SALAD

Makes: 5 cups • Prep time: 20 minutes • Total time: 20 minutes

For the veggies:

2 cups jicama, shredded	1 cup carrot, shredded
1 cup beet, shredded	1 cup sunflower sprouts

For the dressing:

3 Tbsp avocado oil	1 tsp ginger, minced
1-2 Tbsp lime juice	5-10 mint leaves, minced (optional)
1 Tbsp coconut aminos	Black pepper to taste (optional)

Place jicama, beet, carrot, and sunflower sprouts in a large bowl.

In a small bowl, whisk together avocado oil, lime juice, ginger, mint, and salt. Pour the dressing over the veggie mixture and toss to coat. Taste and adjust the flavors according to your preference.

THAI CRUNCH SALAD

Makes: 5 cups • Prep time: 20 minutes • Total time: 20 minutes

For the salad:

2 cups purple cabbage, shredded	1 small cucumber, shredded
1 cup green cabbage, shredded	1 cup mung bean sprouts
2 carrots, shredded	1-2 green onions, sliced

For the dressing:

⅓ cup almond butter	1 Tbsp lime juice
¼ cup water	2 tsp ginger, minced
3 Tbsp coconut aminos or tamari	1 clove garlic, minced

In a bowl, toss together purple and green cabbage, carrot, cucumber, mung bean sprouts, and green onion.

In a small bowl, whisk together almond butter, water, coconut aminos, lime juice, ginger, and garlic. Taste and adjust the flavors according to your preference.

Pour dressing over veggies and toss to coat. Top with sunflower seeds if desired.

Store in a sealed container in the refrigerator for up to two days.

ITALIAN SPROUT SALAD

For the salad:

3 cups lentil sprouts

1 cup chopped spinach or kale

¼ cup sundried tomato, minced

¼ cup olives, chopped

¼ cup red onion, diced small

¼ cup pine nuts or hemp seeds

For the dressing:

⅓ cup olive oil

¼ cup fresh basil, minced

3 Tbsp balsamic vinegar

1 clove garlic, minced

¼ tsp salt

Black pepper to taste

Place all salad ingredients in a bowl and toss together.

In a small bowl, whisk together all dressing ingredients. Pour the dressing over the salad and toss to combine.

Store in a sealed container in the refrigerator for up to two days.

AVOCADO KALE SALAD

Makes: 5 cups • Prep time: 20 minutes • Total time: 20 minutes

For the salad:

1 bunch lacinato kale, finely chopped

2 Tbsp lemon juice

1 Tbsp coconut aminos

1 large avocado, diced

½ cup cherry tomatoes, chopped

¼ cup hemp seeds

For the dressing:

3 Tbsp olive oil

1 Tbsp lemon juice

1 tsp dijon mustard (optional)

1 small clove garlic, minced

¼ tsp salt

Black pepper to taste

Place chopped kale in a bowl, coat with lemon juice and coconut aminos, and massage the kale with your hands until it softens.

In a small bowl, whisk together all dressing ingredients. Pour the dressing over the kale, along with the remaining salad ingredients. Toss to combine.

Top with sunflower sprouts and any herbs you like.

TABBOULEH

Makes: 5 cups • Prep time: 30 minutes • Total time: 30 minutes

½ cup almonds

4 cups cauliflower

¼ cup hemp seeds

1 cup parsley, minced

1 cup cherry tomatoes, seeded and chopped

1 cucumber, seeded and diced

¼ cup red onion, diced small

⅓ cup olive oil

¼ cup lemon juice

½ tsp salt

Black pepper to taste

In a food processor, grind the almonds into crumbs. Add cauliflower and pulse until it reaches the consistency of couscous. Optional: spread cauliflower on a Teflex sheet and dehydrate at 115 °F for 20-30 minutes to remove excess liquid.

Pour mixture into a bowl and stir in all remaining ingredients. Taste and adjust flavors according to your preference.

Top with lentil sprouts for an extra boost of nutrients!

Store in a sealed container in the refrigerator for up to two days.

BROCCOLI SALAD

Makes: 5 cups • Prep time: 20 minutes • Total time: 20 minutes

For the salad:

3 cups broccoli, chopped small
1 ½ cups lentil or mung bean sprouts

1 cup carrot, shredded

For the dressing:

3 Tbsp avocado oil
3 Tbsp coconut aminos
2 Tbsp lemon juice
1-2 Tbsp cajun seasoning

1 small clove garlic, minced
¼ tsp salt
Black pepper to taste

Combine broccoli, sprouts, and carrot in a large bowl.

In a small bowl, whisk together all dressing ingredients. Taste and adjust the flavors according to your preference. Pour dressing over broccoli mixture and toss to coat.

Store in a sealed container in the refrigerator for up to two days.

FAJITAS

Makes: 4 cups • Prep time: 30 minutes • Total time: 8-10 hours

For the mushrooms:

4 portabello mushrooms, sliced

2 Tbsp avocado oil

2 Tbsp tamari

1 tsp cumin

½ tsp chili powder

½ tsp garlic powder

For the peppers and onions:

2 red/yellow bell peppers, sliced

1 small yellow onion, sliced

2 Tbsp avocado oil

2 Tbsp lime juice

1 Tbsp coconut aminos

2 tsp chili powder

In a bowl, mix together all mushroom ingredients. Cover and let marinate in the refrigerator overnight.

In a separate bowl (preferably glass or ceramic), mix together all ingredients for the peppers and onions. Place the bowl in the dehydrator and dehydrate at 105 °F for 8-10 hours, stirring once or twice if possible.

When ready to serve, heat a pan over medium heat and cook the mushrooms for 5-7 minutes. Remove from heat and let cool. Toss together the mushrooms with the peppers and onions.

Serve over a bed of romaine and top with guacamole, if desired.

HOT WINGS

1 medium head of cauliflower

¼ cup coconut aminos

1 cup almonds

1 cup sunflower seeds

¾ cup water

3 Tbsp cajun seasoning

1 Tbsp lemon juice

1 tsp smoked paprika

1 tsp salt

1 tsp garlic powder

½ tsp onion powder

Chop cauliflower into bite-sized florets. Toss with coconut aminos and set aside.

In a food processor, combine all the remaining ingredients and process into a thick, grainy batter.

Pour batter over cauliflower and toss to coat. Spread the cauliflower in a single layer over two Teflex sheets. Dehydrate at 110 °F for 20-22 hours, until crisp on the outside.

Serve with a side of ranch dressing, if desired.

AVOCADO FRIES

Makes: 4 servings · Prep time: 20 minutes · Total time: 2-4 hours

2 medium avocados

⅓ cup flax seeds

⅓ cup cashews

1 Tbsp nutritional yeast

1 tsp garlic powder

½ tsp salt

Slice each avocado into ½-inch wedges. Place in a bowl and set aside.

In a blender, grind flax seeds and cashews into crumbs. Mix in nutritional yeast, garlic powder, and salt. Pour this mixture over the avocados and toss to coat.

Spread avocados into a mesh dehydrator sheet and dehydrate at 110 °F for 2-4 hours.

ONION RINGS

Makes: 4 servings • Prep time: 20 minutes • Total time: 18-20 hours

1 large yellow onion	¼ cup flax seeds
1 Tbsp tamari	1 Tbsp nutritional yeast
½ cup almonds	¼ tsp salt

Slice onion into ¼- to ½-inch thick slices and place in a bowl. Toss with tamari and set aside.

In a blender, grind the almonds, flax, nutritional yeast, and salt into a fine crumb.

Pour mixture over the onions and toss gently to coat (not too much or the coating will start clumping and falling off).

Spread onto a Teflex sheet and dehydrate at 110 °F for 18-20 hours, until crispy.

DRESSINGS

RANCH DRESSING

¾ cup cashews

¾ cup water

2 Tbsp lemon juice

1 Tbsp coconut aminos

½ tsp garlic powder

½ tsp onion powder

¼-½ tsp salt

1 Tbsp fresh parsley, minced

1 Tbsp fresh dill, minced

½ tsp black pepper

In a blender, combine all ingredients except parsley, dill, and black pepper. Blend on high until smooth. Mix in remaining ingredients. Taste and adjust flavors according to your preference.

Serve over a salad of spring mix, shredded carrot, chopped tomato, and sunflower sprouts.

Store in a sealed container in the refrigerator for up to five days.

CAESAR &
THOUSAND ISLAND

Makes: 1 cup • Prep time: 10 minutes • Total time: 10 minutes

Caesar dressing:

¼ cup sunflower seeds

¼ cup cashews

¾ cup water

1 Tbsp capers

1 Tbsp dijon mustard

1 Tbsp lemon juice

1 Tbsp olive oil

Black pepper to taste

In a blender, combine all ingredients except black pepper. Blend on high until smooth. Mix in black pepper. Taste and adjust the flavors according to your preference.

Makes: 1 cup • Prep time: 10 minutes • Total time: 10 minutes

Thousand island dressing:

⅓ cup water

¼ cup cashews

½ cup tomatoes, chopped

2 Tbsp lemon juice

2 Tbsp onion, minced

2 Tbsp dill relish

1 clove garlic, minced

Pinch of salt

In a blender, combine water, cashews, tomatoes, and lemon juice. Blend until smooth. Add onion, relish, and garlic and blend on low to combine, leaving small pieces intact.

SUNNY MUSTARD & LEMON TAHINI

Makes: 1.5 cups • Prep time: 10 minutes • Total time: 10 minutes

Sunny mustard dressing:

⅓ cup sunflower seeds

¾ cup water

3 Tbsp dijon mustard

2 Tbsp coconut aminos

2 Tbsp yellow onion, chopped

½ tsp black pepper (optional)

In a blender, combine all ingredients except black pepper. Blend on high until smooth. Mix in black pepper.

Makes: 1.5 cups • Prep time: 10 minutes • Total time: 10 minutes

Lemon tahini dressing:

½ cup tahini

½ cup water

⅓ cup lemon juice

1 clove garlic, minced

¼ tsp salt

¼ tsp black pepper

In a bowl, whisk together all ingredients until smooth.

STRAWBERRY VINAIGRETTE

1 cup strawberries

1 Medjool date, pitted

⅓ cup lemon juice

½ cup avocado oil

⅛-¼ tsp salt

In a blender, combine strawberries, date, and lemon juice and blend on high until smooth. Add avocado oil and salt and blend on low to combine. Taste and adjust the flavors according to your preference.

Serve over a salad of spinach, shredded beet, sliced red onions, and pecans.

Store in a sealed container in the refrigerator for up to five days.

BALSAMIC VINAIGRETTE & CREAMY ITALIAN

Makes: 1.5 cups • Prep time: 10 minutes • Total time: 10 minutes

Balsamic vinaigrette::

1 cup olive oil	1 tsp dried basil
½ cup balsamic vinegar	½ tsp onion powder
1 clove garlic, minced	¼ tsp black pepper
1 tsp dried oregano	⅛-¼ tsp salt

In a bowl, whisk together all ingredients. Taste and adjust the flavors according to your preference.

Makes: 1.5 cups • Prep time: 10 minutes • Total time: 10 minutes

Creamy Italian dressing:

½ cup water	1 Tbsp red wine vinegar
¼ cup pine nuts	1 clove garlic, minced
¼ cup olive oil	⅛-¼ tsp salt
2 Tbsp lemon juice	1 Tbsp Italian seasoning

In a blender, combine all ingredients except Italian seasoning and blend until smooth. Stir in Italian seasoning. Taste and adjust the flavors according to your preference.

SESAME GINGER & CILANTRO LIME

Makes: 1.5 servings • Prep time: 10 minutes • Total time: 10 minutes

Sesame ginger dressing:

½ cup tahini

½ cup water

⅓ cup lime or lemon juice

2-3 Tbsp coconut aminos

2-3 Tbsp ginger, minced

1 clove garlic, minced

In a bowl, whisk together all ingredients until smooth. Taste and adjust the flavors according to your preference.

Makes: 1.5 cup • Prep time: 10 minutes • Total time: 10 minutes

Cilantro lime dressing:

⅓ cup avocado oil

⅓ cup lime juice

⅓ cup cilantro

¼ cup zucchini

¼ cup yellow onion

⅛-¼ tsp salt

In a bowl, whisk together all ingredients until smooth. Taste and adjust the flavors according to your preference.

CHIMICHURRI

Makes: 1.5 cups • Prep time: 15 minutes • Total time: 15 minutes

⅔ cup avocado oil

⅔ cup cilantro, minced

⅓ cup parsley, minced

⅓ cup lime juice

¼ cup red onion, minced

2 gloves garlic, minced

1 jalapeno, minced (optional)*

¼-½ tsp salt

Place all ingredients in a bowl and whisk together. Alternatively, place all ingredients in a blender and blend medium to combine, leaving some texture. Taste and adjust the flavors according to your preference.

Serve over cauliflower rice with tempeh, and avocado.

Store in a sealed container in the refrigerator for up to five days.

*Minced jalapeno can be replaced with 1 tsp of crushed red pepper.

KETCHUP & BBQ SAUCE

Makes: 1 cup • Prep time: 10 minutes • Total time: 10 minutes

Ketchup:

1 cup tomatoes, chopped

⅓ cup sundried tomatoes

2 Tbsp coconut aminos

1 Tbsp apple cider vinegar

1 clove garlic

¼ tsp onion powder

Place all ingredients in a blender and blend on high until smooth. Taste and adjust the flavors according to your preference.

Makes: 1 cup • Prep time: 10 minutes • Total time: 10 minutes

BBQ sauce:

1 cup tomatoes, chopped

⅓ cup sundried tomatoes

3 Tbsp coconut aminos

1 Tbsp dijon mustard

1 clove garlic

½ tsp smoked paprika

¼ tsp onion powder

¼ tsp garlic powder

¼ tsp chili powder

¼ tsp black pepper

Place all ingredients in a blender and blend on high until smooth. Taste and adjust the flavors according to your preference.

MAYONNAISE &
SOUR CREAM

Makes: 1 cup • Prep time: 10 minutes • Total time: 10 minutes

Mayonnaise:

½ cup cashews

⅓ cup water

¼ cup avocado oil

1 Tbsp lemon juice

¼ tsp salt

Place all ingredients in a blender and blend until smooth. Taste and adjust the flavors according to your preference. Add garlic, basil, or other flavors to make an aioli sauce!

Makes: 1 cup • Prep time: 10 minutes • Total time: 10 minutes

Sour cream:

⅔ cup coconut yogurt

½ cup cashews

1 Tbsp lemon juice

¼ tsp salt

Place all ingredients in a blender and blend until smooth, adding a splash of water if necessary. Taste and adjust the flavors according to your preference.

Store in a sealed container in the refrigertor for up to one week.

MUSHROOM GRAVY

Makes: 1.5 cups • Prep time: 15 minutes • Total time: 15 minutes

1 cup mushrooms

⅓ cup water

3 Tbsp tahini

3 Tbsp yellow onion

3 Tbsp tamari or coconut aminos

1 Tbsp flax seed

1 clove garlic

¼ tsp dried thyme

¼ tsp dried rosemary

¼ tsp black pepper

Salt to taste

Place mushrooms in a saucepan and cover with water. Bring to a boil, then reduce heat and let simmer for 5 minutes. Remove from heat, drain the water off, and allow the mushrooms to cool.

Place all ingredients except herbs in a blender and blend on high until smooth. Add the herbs and blend on low to combine. Taste and adjust the flavors according to your preference.

Store in a sealed container in the refrigerator for up to three days.

SNACKS

DRIED APPLE RINGS

4 granny smith apples, cored
2 Tbsp lemon juice

1 tsp cinnamon (optional)

Using a mandolin, slice apples into thin rings and place in a bowl. Toss with lemon juice and cinnamon.

Spread apple rings in a single layer on mesh dehydrator sheets and dehydrate at 105 °F for 24-48 hours (depending on your preferred texture).

Store in a sealed container at room temperature for up to two weeks.

ZUCCHINI CHIPS

2 medium zuchini

1 tsp avocado oil

1 tsp lemon juice

½ tsp garlic powder

½ tsp salt

Black pepper to taste

Slice the zucchinis into ⅛-inch thick rounds and place in a bowl. Add all remaining ingredients and toss to coat.

Spread in a single layer on a mesh dehydrator sheet and dehydrate at 115 °F for one to two days, until crisp.

Store in a sealed container at room temperature for up to one week.

CRUNCHY SPROUTS

Makes: 4 servings • Prep time: 5 minutes • Total time: 14-18 hours

4 cups lentil sprouts

¼ cup coconut aminos

2 tsp of your favorite seasoning mix

Combine all ingredients in a glass bowl and dehydrate at 110 °F for 14-18 hours, until dried and crunchy.

Store in a sealed container at room temperature for up to two weeks.

KALE CHIPS

Makes: 4 trays • Prep time: 20 minutes • Total time: 18-20 hours

2 bunches of kale

1 ½ cups cashews

¾ cup water

¼ cup nutritional yeast

2 Tbsp lemon juice

2 cloves garlic

1 ½ tsp salt

Wash kale, remove stems, and rip into pieces about the size of the palm of your hand. Place in a large bowl and set aside.

In a high-power blender, combine all remaining ingredients and blend on high until smooth.

Pour the batter over the kale and use your hands to massage it into all the nooks and crannies. Spread the kale in a single layer on Teflex sheets and dehydrate at 115 °F for 18-20 hours, until completely dry and crispy.

These kale chips are hearty and crunchy. For a lighter version, try using only lemon juice and salt.

Store in a sealed container at room temperature for up to one week. If they start to lose their crispness, return them to the dehydrator for 1 hour.

STICKY NUTS

Makes: 8 servings • Prep time: 2 minutes • Total time: 24-26 hours

2 cups nuts of your choice

3 Tbsp coconut aminos

In a glass bowl, mix together nuts and coconut aminos. Place bowl in the dehydrator and dehydrate at 110 °F for 24-26 hours, stirring once after the first few hours, and again towards the end.

Play around with this recipe by adding some of your favorite seasonings!

Store in a sealed container at room temperature for up to two weeks.

EVERYTHING AVOCADO

1 large avocado   1 Tbsp "everything bagel" seasoning

Cut avocado in half and remove the pit. Coat each half with "everything bagel" seasoning (and a pinch of salt, if not included in the seasoning).

"Everything bagel" seasoning can be substituted with any seasoning of your choice.

ENERGY CHUNKS

Makes: 9 squares • Prep time: 15 minutes • Total time: 1 hour

¾ cup almonds

½ cup Brazil nuts

2 Tbsp hemp seeds

¼ cup coconut butter

1 Medjool date, pitted

2 Tbsp goji berries

1 tsp vanilla

½ tsp maca Powder

Pinch salt

In a food processor, process nuts and hemp seeds into a coarse crumb. Add coconut butter and date, process until fully incorporated.

Add remaining ingredients and pulse to combine, leaving little pieces of goji berries intact.

Gather mixture into a ball and transfer to a clean, flat surface. Shape mixture into a square, about 1-inch thick. Cut into nine equal pieces and refrigerate for 1 hour to set.

Store in a sealed container in the refrigerator for up to two weeks.

FRUIT ROLL UP

2 cups berries   ¼ cup chia seeds

In a blender, blend berries and chia seeds until smooth. Let sit for about 10 minutes to thicken.

Spread the mixture in a ⅛-inch layer on Teflex sheets and dehydrate at 105 °F for 12-14 hours, until dry yet pliable.

Cut the dried fruit into strips and roll them up. Store in a sealed container in the refrigerator for up to one week.

DESSERTS

BROWNIES

1 cup almonds

1 cup walnuts or pecans

4 Medjool dates, pitted

⅓ cup cacao powder

2 Tbsp coconut butter

⅛-¼ tsp salt

Place nuts in a food processor and process into fine crumbs. Add remaining ingredients and process until thoroughly combined.

Press mixture into the bottom of a small square pan, then slice into 9 pieces.

Chill in the refrigerator for at least 1 hour, or overnight.

Store in a sealed container in the refrigerator for up to two weeks.

CINNAMON CRUMBLE

Makes: 9 servings • Prep time: 30 minutes • Total time: 1-2 hours

For the base:

1 ½ cups almonds

1 cup cashews

4 Medjool dates, pitted

¼ cup coconut butter

1 ½ tsp vanilla

1 tsp maca powder

⅛-¼ tsp salt

For the crumble:

1 cup pecans

1 cup walnuts

2 Tbsp cinnamon

2-3 Tbsp maple syrup

Pinch of salt

To make the base, combine almonds and cashews in a food processor and grind into a flour. Add remaining ingredients and process to combine. Pour mixture onto a baking sheet and divide in two. Flatten each mound into equal-sized squares, about ½-inch thick. Place in the refrigerator to chill while you prepare the crumble.

To make the crumble, combine all ingredients in a food processor and pulse into a crumbly texture. Divide mixture in two and gently press one half onto one of your base layers. Carefully pick up the second base layer using a spatula or dough scraper and stack on top of the crumble layer. Place remaining half of the crumble mixture on top of the cake and gently press together.

Chill in the refrigerator for at least 1 hour, or overnight.

STRAWBERRY CAKE

Makes: 16 servings · Prep time: 25 minutes · Total time: 1-2 hours

For the cake:

1 ½ cups pecans	2 cups frozen strawberries
1 ½ cups walnuts	4 Medjool dates, pitted
¼ cup hemp seeds	½ tsp vanilla
½ cup coconut butter	⅛-¼ tsp salt

For the topping:

1 cup pecans	1 Tbsp date syrup
1 cup gluten-free rolled oats	2 tsp cinnamon
¼ cup shredded coconut	Pinch salt

To make the cake, combine nuts and hemp seeds in a food processor and process into a coarse crumb. Add coconut butter and pulse to incorporate. Add remaining ingredients and process until mostly smooth. Press mixture into an 8" x 8" pan and set aside.

To make the topping, place all ingredients in a food processor and pulse to crumble. Pour crumble topping onto the cake and place in the refrigerator for at least 1 hour to set.

Cover and store in the refrigerator for up to five days.

CARROT CAKE

Makes: 16 servings • Prep time: 30 minutes • Total time: 1-2 hours

For the cake:

1 cup almonds	2 cups carrot, shredded
1 cup walnuts	1 ½ tsp cinnamon
1 cup pecans	½ tsp vanilla extract
½ cup cashews	¼ tsp nutmeg
¼ cup hemp seeds	Pinch cloves (optional)
6 Medjool dates, pitted	⅛-¼ tsp salt

For the frosting:

1 cup macadamia nuts	¼ cup maple syrup
¼ cup coconut butter	½ tsp vanilla
⅓ cup water	Pinch of salt
1 Tbsp lemon juice	

To make the cake, place nuts and hemp seeds in a food processor and grind into a fine crumb. Add dates and process to combine. Add remaining ingredients and process to combine, leaving some texture. Spread mixture into an 8" x 8" cake pan and set aside.

To make the frosting, combine all ingredients in a blender and blend until smooth. Spread the frosting over cake and place in the refrigerator for 1-2 hours to set.

Cover and store in the refrigerator for up to five days.

CINNAMON ROLLS

Makes: 12 servings • Prep time: 1.5 hours • Total time: 8-10 hours

For the dough:

½ cup almonds

½ cup walnuts

1 cup golden flax seed

½ cup young Thai coconut meat

2 Medjool dates, pitted

2 cups water

¼ tsp salt

For the filling:

1 cup pecans

¼ cup cinnamon

8 Medjool dates, pitted

¼ cup almond milk

¼ tsp salt

In a blender, grind almonds, walnuts, and flax into a flour. Pour into a bowl and set aside. Place coconut meat, dates, water, and salt into the blender and blend on high until smooth. Add the nut flour back into the blender and blend to combine.

Divide mixture in two and portion onto two Teflex sheets. Using a cake spatula or dough scraper, spread mixture out into rectangles, about 8" x 11" and ¼-inch thick. Dehydrate at 105 °F for 7-9 hours, flipping every 2-3 hours, until dry but pliable.

In a food processor, grind pecans and cinnamon into a coarse flour. Pour into a bowl and set aside. In the food processor, blend dates, almond milk, and salt into a paste. Add pecan mixture back into the food processor and pulse to combine.

Carefully spread onto the dough sheets. Roll the dough sheets into logs and slice each log into 6 equal segments.

CHEESECAKE

Makes: 12 servings • Prep time: 30 minutes • Total time: 18-20 hours

For the crust:

½ cup almonds

½ cup pecans

½ cup gluten-free rolled oats

1 Medjool date, pitted

1 Tbsp coconut butter

½ tsp maca powder (optional)

Pinch of salt

For the filling:

1 cup cashews, soaked

¾ cup coconut yogurt

¼ cup coconut butter

4 Medjool dates, pitted

1 tsp vanilla extract

Pinch salt

To make the crust, place nuts and oats in a food processor and grind into a fine crumb. Add remaining ingredients and process until thoroughly combined. It should stick together when pressed between your fingers. Press the mixture into a 7" springform pan (or two 4" springform pans) and set aside.

To make the filling, place all ingredients in a high-power blender and blend until smooth and creamy. This is a very thick mixture, so you may have to use your blender's tamper tool. Pour the filling over the crust and freeze (uncovered) overnight to set.

Thaw the cheesecake for 10 minutes before slicing and serving.

Cover and store in the freezer for up to two weeks.

COCONUT CREAM PIE

Makes: 12 servings • Prep time: 40 minutes • Total time: 9+ hours

For the crust:

1 cup almonds	2 Medjool dates, pitted
1 cup walnuts	2 Tbsp coconut butter
½ cup gluten-free rolled oats	¼ tsp salt

For the filling:

2 cups young Thai coconut meat*	½ cup coconut cream
¾ cup young Thai coconut water	2 tsp vanilla extract
¼ cup coconut butter	⅛-¼ tsp salt
4 Medjool dates, pitted	

To make the crust, place nuts and oats in a food processor and grind into a flour. Add the dates, coconut butter, and salt and process to combine. Press the mixture into the bottom and sides of a 9" pie dish and set aside.

To make the filling, place coconut meat, coconut water, dates, and coconut butter in a high-power blender and blend on high until completely smooth. This may take a few minutes, and you may have to use your blender's tamper tool. Add the remaining ingredients and blend on low to combine.

Pour mixture into prepared pie crust and refrigerate for at least 8 hours, or overnight.

*3-4 young Thai coconuts usually yields about 2 cups.

APPLE PIE

Makes: 5 servings · Prep time: 40 minutes · Total time: 40 minutes

For the crust:

1 cup almonds	¼ cup coconut butter
1 cup pecans	2 Medjool dates, pitted
1 cup gluten free rolled oats	¼ tsp salt

For the filling:

2 green apples, peeled and cored	2-3 tsp cinnamon
¾ cup cashews, soaked	¼ tsp nutmeg
¼ cup water	¼ tsp ground ginger
2 Tbsp maple syrup	Pinch of salt

To make the crust, place nuts and oats in a food processor and grind into a flour. Add remaining ingredients and process until combined. Pour ⅔ of the mixture into a 9" pie dish and press the mixture into the bottom and sides. Place in the refrigerator while you prepare the filling. Set the remaining mixture aside.

To make the filling, cut the apples into quarters and slice them thinly. Place them in a bowl and set aside.

In a high-power blender, combine all remaining ingredients and blend on high until smooth. Pour cashew mixture over apples and toss to combine. Spread evenly into pie pan and top with remaining crust mixture.

OATMEAL RAISIN COOKIE

Makes: 12 servings • Prep time: 20 minutes • Total time: 1 hour

½ cup almonds

⅓ cup cashews

¼ cup walnuts

¼ cup coconut butter

4 Medjool dates, pitted

1 ¼ cup gluten-free rolled oats

2 Tbsp water

1-2 tsp cinnamon

⅛-¼ tsp salt

¼ cup raisins

In a food processor, process nuts into a flour. Add coconut butter and dates, and process to combine. Add all remaining ingredients except raisins and pulse until combined. Stir in raisins.

Portion mixture into cookie-sized mounds (about 2 Tbsp each) on a tray and press each mound firmly with the palm of your hand, shaping the sides as you go.

Refrigerate the cookies for at least 30 minutes to set.

Store in a sealed container in the refrigerator for up to two weeks.

COCONUT-CASHEW COOKIES

Makes: 16 servings • Prep time: 20 minutes • Total time: 16-18 hours

1 cup cashews

1 cup shredded coconut (unsweetened)

1-2 Medjool dates, pitted

1 Tbsp coconut butter

1 tsp vanilla extract

Pinch of salt

In a food processor, grind cashews and shredded coconut until it begins to clump together. Add dates and process until combined. Add remaining ingredients and process once more.

Using a cookie dough scooper, portion dough out onto a plate or tray. Flatten each cookie with the palm of your hand.

Transfer to a mesh dehydrator screen and dehydrate at 110 °F for 16-18 hours.

Store in a sealed container in the refrigerator for up to two weeks.

PUDDING: TWO WAYS

Makes: 4 servings • Prep time: 15 minutes • Total time: 15 minutes

Vanilla coconut pudding:

1½ cups young Thai coconut meat	½ tsp vanilla
¾ cup young Thai coconut water	Pinch of salt
1 Medjool date, pitted	

Chocolate avocado pudding:

2 large avocados	½ tsp vanilla
¼ cup cacao powder	Pinch salt
2 Tbsp maple syrup	

The instructions for both recipes are the same: place all ingredients in a blender and blend on high until smooth.

The vanilla coconut pudding can be stored in a sealed container in the refrigerator for up to five days.

The chocolate avocado pudding should be served immediately.

ABOUT THE AUTHORS

Dr. Thomas Lodi has always been something of an enigma within the oncology community challenging the status quo. When he first established An Oasis of Healing in 2005, his alternative and nutritional solutions for healing cancer were viewed as radical. At the time, few if any other centers provided a comprehensive mix of conventional and alternative medicine to help patients heal. Dr. Thomas Lodi added to the medical components, an organic raw vegan diet, whole body cleansing, and mind/body healing. Dr. Lodi pioneered an integrative cancer treatment approach which has now become the definitive route for those unsatisfied with the modern medical cancer treatment system. Current day, many other doctors, facilities, and patients have adopted his approach and methods into their cancer treatment programs. His cancer treatments have revolutionized the integrative side of the cancer industry worldwide and led many patients with cancer to the root of true healing and health restoration.

Thomas Lodi has been practicing medicine for over 35 years. Prior to attending medical school, Dr. Lodi practiced as a clinical psychologist during which time he was director of psychological services for a 240 bed in patient facility in Hawaii.

After graduating from the University of Hawaii School of Medicine in 1985, Dr. Lodi served as a visiting Clinical Fellow at Columbia University College of Physicians and Surgeons in New York City, where he also underwent training in Internal Medicine. From 1991 to 1996, Dr. Lodi was appointed as Clinical Instructor of Medicine at the University of Hawaii School of Medicine.

For the first ten years of his medical career, Dr. Thomas Lodi worked in conventional settings as an internal medicine specialist, urgent care physician, and as an intensivist in ICU and CCU departments of various hospitals.

After he read the book Medical Miracle: Hydrogen Peroxide, his whole perspective on medicine shifted and he began a lifelong search for more effective and less toxic cancer therapies trainings around the world including Japan, Germany, Mexico, Malaysia, Thailand, and all throughout the United States.

Dr. Thomas Lodi maintains memberships in both conventional and alternative medical professional associations in order to remain current in all areas of oncology for the benefit of his patients. He is licensed as an Integrative and Homeopathic Medical Doctor (MDH) in the State of Arizona and he is licensed as an Allopathic Medical Doctor (MD) in the state of New York. Dr. Lodi has completed a Fellowship in Integrative Cancer Therapies and a Fellowship in Anti-Aging, Regenerative & Functional Medicine. Dr. Lodi sits on the Scientific Advisory Board for Immunogenic Research Foundation (IMREF), the Medical Advisory Board for IOIP, International Organization for Integrative Physicians, and is an active-allied member of the American Society of Clinical Oncology (ASCO). Dr. Lodi is also an instructor in Insulin Potentiation Therapy and certified in oxidative and chelation therapies.

The rather direct stance Dr. Lodi takes regarding empowering his patients to understand their body's ability to heal through the School of Life education program may leave some disconcerted at first. His entire purpose for the School of Life is to ensure patients graduate the program at An Oasis of Healing with the tools, knowledge, and understanding of how to guide their own healing and health care.

An Oasis of Healing is a holistic cancer healing center that was established in Mesa, Arizona in 2005. Our Comprehensive Cancer Care Program integrates proven science based alternative and natural therapies with the most effective and least harmful mainstream medicines to heal and eradicate cancer in the body. The foundation of our program provides the nutrition and cleansing required for patients to change the biochemistry of their body so that it stops making cancer.

For 17 years, An Oasis of Healing has been the leading cancer center in the United States with a holistic and fully integrative approach that has all aspects required for healing cancer in one location. Our approach incorporates highly dense nutrition through living foods and fresh-pressed juices, enhancement therapies for cleansing and detoxification with alternative and natural intravenous treatments – all of which, along with conventional medicines, both target and eliminate cancer while rebuilding and strengthening the immune system. We provide the most comprehensive program for dealing with the complexities of cancer while addressing the whole person throughout the healing process including physical, emotional, mental, and spiritual well-being.

We empower and inspire our patients and their caregivers by providing the tools and knowledge required for them to be active participants in the healing journey. We provide a caring and encouraging atmosphere filled with passion and hope.

We invite you to find out more and sign up for our newsletter at:
www.AnOasisOfHealing.com or www.StopMakingCancer.com

If you or a loved one has been diagnosed with cancer, please call us to discover how we can help at 480-834-5414.

Printed in the USA
CPSIA information can be obtained
at www.ICGtesting.com
CBHW042332010824
12557CB00058B/965

9 781662 932779